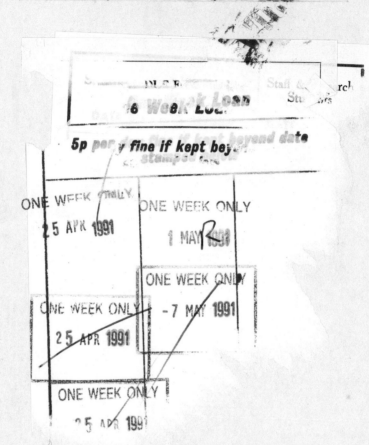

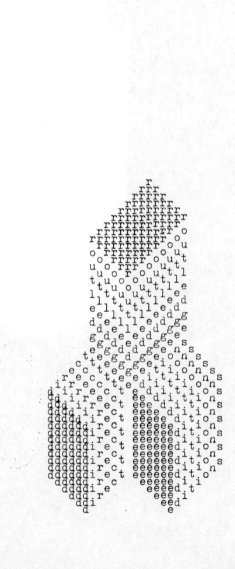

THE CAUSES OF INDUSTRIAL DISORDER
A comparison of a British and a German factory

Ian Maitland

ROUTLEDGE DIRECT EDITIONS

ROUTLEDGE & KEGAN PAUL
London, Boston, Melbourne and Henley

First published in 1983
by Routledge & Kegan Paul Ltd
39 Store Street, London WC1E 7DD,
9 Park Street, Boston, Mass. 02108, USA,
296 Beaconsfield Parade, Middle Park,
Melbourne 3206, Australia, and
Broadway House, Newtown Road,
Henley-on-Thames, Oxon RG9 1EN
Printed in Great Britain by
The Thetford Press Ltd,
Thetford, Norfolk

Library of Congress Cataloging in Publication Data

Maitland, Ian.
The causes of industrial disorder.

(Routledge direct editions)
Bibliography: p.146.
Includes index.
1. Industrial relations--Great Britain.
2. Industrial relations--Germany (West).
3. Comparative management. I. Title.
HD8391.M294   331'.0941   82-7516
ISBN 0-7100-9207-5   AACR2

CONTENTS

ACKNOWLEDGMENTS

I wish to thank the many people in England and Germany who patiently bore my constant prying and who showed me many kindnesses that I will not be able to repay. This book would not have been possible without Allan Silver's intellectual stimulation and moral support. I am also indebted to James W.Kuhn and Andrew Beveridge. Columbia University's Institute on Western Europe generously provided some financial support. My parents know how great a debt I owe them.

Ian Maitland

Chapter 1

DISORDER IN BRITISH INDUSTRY

THE NATURE OF INDUSTRIAL DISORDER

This book presents the findings of a study of the causes of order and disorder in industry. The study was designed to examine three hypotheses: first, that the disorder in British industry is a result of the breakdown of 'government' in the workplace; second, that this breakdown is itself a consequence of the structure of labor relations in Britain; and third, that this disorder has contributed to Britain's relative economic decline. The approach adopted for this purpose was a comparative case-study of a British factory and a similar German one.

The decision to make the workplace my unit of analysis was dictated by the nature of the disorder in British industry. As have many studies before and since, in 1968 a Royal Commission reported that the principal defect in Britain's labor relations was the 'disorder in factory and workshop relations and pay structures' (Donovan, 1968). Therefore a research site was chosen that permitted the observation of labor relations at workplace level in Britain and Germany.

Disorder is not to be confused with the incidence of strikes - though that may be one of its manifestations; rather it is a property of everyday relations on the shop floor. In the sense employed here, disorder means a breakdown of stable patterns for the integration of social behavior - what Parsons calls a 'stable system of social interaction.' In other words, it implies the absence of a set of norms or expectations that enables participants in a social system to orient their behavior so that it is complementary with that of other participants. Where such norms are absent, collective action becomes problematic - in the limiting case, impossible.

In Britain, more than in other countries, everyday relations on the shop floor are marked by constant friction; even in comparatively trivial matters managers commonly have to bargain for the cooperation of workers; workers are likely to use threats or the actual disruption of production as a first resort in order to force a resolution of their grievances; the introduction of new equipment, product models, or work methods is routinely obstructed; job

demarcations are inflexible and workers are likely to resist re-
assignment to other work; and so on. In short, in Britain workers'
compliance - with the wishes of managers, with the requirements of
efficient production, and with the demands of technological change -
is often questionable or conditional.

ALTERNATIVE EXPLANATIONS OF THE DISORDER IN BRITISH INDUSTRY

Why are British labor relations so disordered? Why are German labor
relations, by contrast, relatively free of disorder? At the end of
this chapter I outline the general nature of the answer that will be
offered in this book.
    Before giving my own answer, I critically examine in turn a
number of alternative explanations of the disorder in British industry; and I indicate why I find each of them wanting.

A neo-Durkheimian theory of industrial order: Goldthorpe

In what might be termed a neo-Durkheimian view, industrial order is
possible only if it is rooted in shared moral values. In his attack
on utilitarianism Durkheim had argued that no lasting social arrangements could be founded purely on self-interest:
    Where interest is the only ruling force, each individual finds
    himself in a state of war with every other ... and any truce
    would not be of long duration. There is nothing less constant
    than interest. Today, it unites me to you; tomorrow it will
    make me your enemy. Such a cause can only give rise to transient
    relations and passing associations.
    What promise does this perspective hold for explaining the con-
trasting experiences of British and German labor relations? It
directs our attention to the relative degree of value consensus in
the two countries. Presumably the greater industrial order in
Germany rests on a broader and deeper consensus than exists in
Britain.
    If a common value system is a prerequisite for orderly labor re-
lations then these two countries present a paradox. For it has been
common among consensus theorists to cite Britain as a case of a
culture that exhibits a 'persisting pattern ... of embracing values
and beliefs concerning the peaceful compromise of political differences' (Rose, 1964, p.58; see also Eckstein, 1962, p.73). Mean-
while Germany's political culture has been singled out as one
lacking in the essential overarching consensus vital to sustain
democratic order. According to Almond and Verba (1965, pp.364,362),
Germany's political culture is still not hospitable to 'an effective
and stable democratic political system.' It lacks two essential
ingredients of the 'civic culture:' first, a commitment to the political system and, second, an adequate level of social and inter-
personal trust. Another writer has remarked on the insufficient
'degree of agreement on the all-important rules of the political
game' (Spiro, 1962, p.567). Almond and Verba contrast the relative
absence of 'social norms and trust and confidence' in Germany with
'the values of community and polity in Britain ... that mitigate

partisan cleavage.' In Britain 'fragmentation is impeded by the
force of shared social values and attitudes, which permeate all
aspects of society' (op.cit., pp.313,243).

On the strength of consensus theory, then, we would expect
British labor relations to be more harmonious than Germany's. In
British industry we would expect the incidence of conflict to be
rarer because of the climate of trust characterizing personal relations; we would expect conflict, when it did happen, to be more
orderly because regulated by the existence of norms governing its
expression; and finally, we would expect the intensity of conflict
to be moderated by the existence of a wide range of other values
uniting management and labor. Since these expectations plainly are
not fulfilled, the neo-Durkheimian approach would appear to hold out
little promise for explaining the disorder in British industry.

Let us consider in detail one ambitious attempt to show that the
disorder in British labor relations has its roots in the breakdown
of value consensus. In his essay 'Social inequality and social
integration in modern Britain' (1974a; see also 1974b; 1978),
Goldthorpe argues that this disorder is intelligible in the light
of the anomie in British economic life. This anomie - the lack of
adequate normative regulation of labor relations - is the result of
'the absence of an accepted moral basis for [British] economic
life.' In Goldthorpe's view, 'a relatively stable normative order
in economic life can only be created through norms being underpinned
by some minimum degree of value-consensus.' But no such consensus
is likely so long as British society is 'characterized by the
present marked degree of inequality.'

In other words, so long as the distribution of income and wealth
in Britain has no accepted moral basis, workers will feel no sense
of obligation to restrain their own demands. In the absence of this
moral basis to the structure of earnings there can be no 'moral
regulation to the wants and goals that individuals hold' (1974a,
p.222). In these conditions there is no source of proportion or
stability that might moderate wage demands; and the resulting unrestrained pursuit of economic self-interest by British workers produces industrial disorder.

It should be noted that Goldthorpe is careful to distinguish between class struggle and anomie. In his (1974) writings at least,
he does not argue that the inequalities in Britain have given rise
to a collective, class-based opposition to the economic organization
of British society. In fact he does not even claim that workers
feel a sense of grievance. The source of the disorder is not out-
raged morality but the absence of morality. For a modern industrial
society to be viable it is insufficient that workers should feel no
resentment; such a society must be able to engage their active
moral consent. If a disruptive wages free-for-all is to be held in
check, workers must feel a moral commitment to the established economic order; and no such commitment is likely in conditions of il-
legitimate inequality. In a later piece (1978, p.201), Goldthorpe
adds the stronger claim that the decay of the 'status order' (i.e.,
traditional beliefs legitimating class inequalities) has released
'distributional dissent and conflict at a new level of intensity -
reflecting [a] ... rational appreciation of the nature of class
inequalities.'

Does Goldthorpe's version of the neo-Durkheimian approach bring us any closer to explaining why Britain's labor relations are more disordered than Germany's? Its first obvious difficulty is the imputed link between disorder and inequality. On a variety of indices Britain appears to be among the most egalitarian of advanced industrial societies. (1) Following the logic of Goldthorpe's explanation we might have expected British labor relations to be among the least prone to disorder.

The second issue is the extent to which there exists a value consensus in Britain that might furnish the necessary regulation of economic life. On this point there is evidence from a variety of sources that permits a partial test of Goldthorpe's hypothesis of a breakdown of value consensus. First, what does the literature on British workers' beliefs and attitudes tell us about how they view the unequal distribution of income and wealth in Britain? Specifically, how do they see their own position in this unequal distribution? have their aspirations escalated now that they are no longer held in check by a sense of place in a legitimate structure of earnings? and, finally, is there any indication of intensified distributional conflict? In a national sample survey (conducted in 1962), Runciman (1966) (2) found that only 60 per cent of his respondents gave an affirmative answer to the question 'Do you think there are other sorts of people doing noticeably better at the moment than you and your family?' Moreover, among those who answered in the affirmative, manual workers were most likely to cite other manual groups, while non-manuals mentioned other non-manuals. From these and other data, Runciman concluded that the less well-off tend to use very narrow comparative reference groups when they evaluate their earnings. It has been claimed that since Runciman's study 'the range of comparisons and expectations of production workers has increased' (Hirsch, 1978, p.171). But this claim is not supported by two recent replications of Runciman's study (Daniel, 1976; Scase, 1974; 1977). Daniel formed 'no evidence of either a growing sense of relative deprivation or a widening of comparative reference groups.' There was 'little change in the way people see and evaluate their own position (compared to Runciman in 1962)' and 'little spontaneous demand for the redistribution of earnings across broad occupational categories.' As a result, he concluded, 'such redistribution would in itself provide no solution to any problem of pressure or pay. Neither is it necessary to allay any general feelings of injustice in society' (op. cit., pp.20,24,26). Scase also found virtually no change in the scope of workers' reference groups; and, in comparison with a matched sample of Swedish workers, who are among the least strike-prone in Europe, English workers were more than twice as likely to claim that they could think of no people better off than workers like themselves; moreover, of those who said there were people better off, 76 per cent of the English workers mentioned various manual occupations compared to 44 per cent of the Swedish workers. As Hyman and Brough (1975, p.43), from a Marxist standpoint, have concluded, 'the finding that manual workers tend to compare their earnings with those of other manual workers ... suggests that the existing hierarchy of incomes is generally regarded as normal and natural.' (3) It is worth recalling, too, that 69 per cent of

Goldthorpe et al.'s own sample of affluent workers considered that class inequalities were a necessary feature of society (1968, p. 154).

Another survey finding that has been replicated on several occasions concerns workers' perceptions of their relationship with their employers. This is what Mann (1973) has called the 'football team analogy' in which workers are asked whether employers and workers are on the same side or on different sides. The majority of workers reply 'the same side' (Goldthorpe et al., 1968, p.73 (67 per cent); Cotgrove and Vamplew, 1972 (70 per cent); Wedderburn and Crompton, 1972 (80 per cent); Lane and Roberts, 1971 (69 per cent)). (The workers in the Lane and Roberts sample were on strike at the time of the survey.) (4) Gallie (1978, p.119) found that, in the refineries he studied in France and Britain, 'the British workers ... had an image of the firm that was essentially "cooperative," while the French workers had an image that was essentially exploitative.'

When we turn to workers' views on the state of British labor relations, we find that a surprising number believe that unions have too much power. Parkin (1972, p.93) cites a 1969 poll finding that 67 per cent of union respondents agreed that the activities of their leaders were a 'threat to the prosperity of the country.' The view that unions have too much power was held by 43 per cent of Goldthorpe et al.'s affluent workers (1968, p.26), by 55 per cent of McKenzie and Silver's sample (1968, p.127), by nearly half of the respondents from union households in Butler and Stokes's survey (1969, p.167), and it was disagreed with by only 33 per cent of Cannon's sample of skilled workers (1967, p.168). On the subject of the conduct of labor relations in the workplace, British workers appear to be strong believers in procedure and constitutionality. Flanders (1970, p.308) cites a survey finding that 62 per cent of non-conservative voters favored making wildcat strikes illegal. Cousins (1972) found that only 21 per cent of the shipyard workers he surveyed felt that it was not wrong to strike before the agreed procedure for the settlement of grievances was exhausted.

These examples could be multiplied but they would not alter the picture of substantial consensus in support of the prevailing economic institutions. After reviewing similar evidence Hyman and Brough (1975, p.62) commented that it 'points to a degree of normative consensus underlying both the arguments and the actual practice of [British labor]. Furthermore, the values which are generally embraced tend implicitly or explicitly to underwrite the inequalities of power and material advantage in industry.'

All too plainly the workers' attitudes reported here do not restrain or regulate their behavior sufficiently to preserve order in British industry. Goldthorpe's rejoinder, therefore, might be that these attitudes reveal a largely instrumental orientation to British economic institutions; that this consensus is largely pragmatic, self-interested, calculating, secular, and therefore incapable of inspiring the sort of internalized check that is required.

But if the degree of support and consent revealed in these surveys is inadequate, one is bound to ask what degree of consent would suffice and is it likely to be forthcoming in any liberal society?

Still more to the point, in view of the extraordinarily high threshold of commitment that is apparently required, is it realistic to expect that industrial order must be based on value consensus and on that alone? Are there not other mechanisms or institutions that may sustain industrial order in tandem with a given level of value consensus - or even in its absence? (5) In other words, does the evidence not call into question the proposition that shared values are a sufficient or even a necessary condition of economic order?

Goldthorpe would apparently reject such a possibility. For him enduring 'normative order in economic life can *only* be created through norms being underpinned by some minimum degree of value consensus' (1974a, p.231). Thus he discounts the possibility that coercion could supply the basis for any form of lasting order: 'To the extent that the normative order is imposed by superior power, fundamental discontent and unrest persist if only in latent form' (ibid., p.225). Similarly, he argues that restraint based on custom is less effective than moral discipline.

However, the evidence from Germany casts doubt on the theory that a pragmatic acceptance of the norms of economic life is inherently unstable. Observers of Germany are virtually unanimous in stressing the instrumentalism, pragmatism, and materialism that inform German social relations - particularly in economic and political life. Thus Goldman (1973, p.588) finds that 'public values seem to be largely missing, or at least poorly articulated.... There is a marked absence of any ideological commitment or vision. A kind of prosaic political culture has resulted.' Edinger (1968, p.119) identifies the dominant social value patterns as 'mutual distrust, the desire for privatization, the self-centered materialistic callousness.' Sturmthal (1964, p.68) notes the appeal of 'something vaguely akin to business unionism ... to the younger men who have little ideological attachment to the movement.' Nickel (1978) notes the similarities between the attitudes of German workers to their unions and those found by Goldthorpe et al. among their affluent workers. Dahrendorf (1969, p.418) finds that in Germany 'a world of highly individual values has emerged which puts the experienced happiness of the individual in first place and increasingly lets the so-called whole slip from sight.' In short, an instrumental orientation is no less characteristic - probably more so - of the German worker than of the British. Accordingly, if such an orientation inhibits active moral commitment to the norms of economic life - without which they are ineffective - then that commitment must be absent in Germany as well and apparently without any ill-effects for industrial order.

In summary, then, a neo-Durkheimian approach to the problem of order in labor relations appears to hold out little heuristic promise. If the degree of national value consensus were the crucial variable, we should expect British labor relations to be more orderly. Goldthorpe's refinement of this approach does not improve its explanatory power. His argument is contradicted by the contrasting experiences of Britain and Germany; German labor relations are more peaceful in spite of both the greater degree of social inequality in Germany and the prevalence of instrumental attitudes among the workforce.

A pluralist explanation of industrial order: Dahrendorf

I turn now to a family of critiques of the institutions of German
politics and labor relations that may loosely be grouped together
under the rubric of pluralist theories. What the authors of these
critiques - mostly interest group pluralists or sociological conflict theorists - have in common is a belief in the salutary effects
of the free play of group conflict; and they charge that Germany
has only grudgingly and half-heartedly accepted that social conflict
is an intrinsic part of democratic politics.
     For such critics conflict is the life breath of a democratic
system; indeed in its absence a political culture hospitable to
democratic politics is likely to atrophy. For example, Lipset
(1963, pp.2,3) argues that the 'consensus on the norms of tolerance
which a society or organization accepts has often developed only as
a result of basic conflict, and requires the continuation of conflict to sustain it.' Accordingly, 'cleavage - where it is legitimate - contributes to the integration of societies and organizations. Trade unions, for example, help to integrate their members
in the larger body politic and give them a basis of loyalty to the
system.' It is evident, particularly from the latter remark, that
this is a theory not only of democracy but also of the conditions
for social order. This point is also apparent in Coser's discussion
of the functions of conflict for social cohesion (1956). In this
view, conflict is not antagonistic to social order; on the contrary, as Dubin (1954) observes in his discussion of collective bargaining, 'the function of conflict is to establish a new basis of
order, not to continue disorder.' The free expression of conflict
between groups is seen as permitting a constant re-equilibration of
their relations in response to changing circumstances. It also
generates the necessary institutions for its own regulation as the
parties involved work out procedures for resolving their differences with the least mutual disruption.
     For the purposes of this discussion certain features of this per-
spective need to be emphasized. First, as we have seen, conflict is
viewed as evoking the means for its own containment. Few would sub-
scribe to a mechanical view of this process, but to some degree this
self-equilibrating tendency is a premise of all these theories. (6)
Second, and related to the first point, the equilibrium is generally
achieved by the opposing parties themselves, without the intervention of third parties, e.g., the state, independent arbitrators,
etc. Third, conflict is a continuous - or at least a periodic -
process, and by permitting successive marginal or incremental adjustments in response to shifts in the underlying power relations
it forestalls much larger dislocations.
     It is no accident that the features enumerated here bear a marked
resemblance to Anglo-Saxon conceptions of collective bargaining, in
particular, and to the operation of interest group pluralism, in
general. It goes without saying, however, that not all these points
receive equal emphasis in all exponents of the pluralist perspective.
     One theorist who does share all these assumptions is Dahrendorf
(1959, 1969). Dahrendorf is of particular interest to the present
discussion because he has explicitly drawn on this perspective to

criticize aspects of German labor relations. These criticisms are
part of a wider critique of German society, so it is appropriate
to begin with that. At the heart of Dahrendorf's critique is the
charge that German society has failed to reconcile itself to the
necessity of conflict. German society is still ill at ease with
the open expression of conflict; its institutions betray a tendency
to hanker after ultimate - and therefore impossible - solutions to
the problem of conflict. The failure to recognize the positive
functions of conflict endangers the survival of German society:
'German society has not yet accepted the reality of conflict and the
necessity of its rational regulation. Many of the most striking
changes in the structure of the economy and society in the Federal
Republic are therefore most liable to be undone again' (1969, p.423;
first German edition 1965). 'The crucial factor for effectively
regulating conflict is recognition, and even emphasis, of systematic
divergence and opposition. The attempt to obliterate lines of conflict by ready ideologies of harmony and unity in effect serves to
increase rather than decrease the violence of conflict manifestations' (1959, pp.225-6).

In this spirit Dahrendorf attacks the German failure to develop
'a modern and liberal system of industrial relations' (1969, pp.
169-70). In particular he criticizes the institutions of the works
council and co-determination for their tendency to blur or gloss
over the fundamental conflicts of interest between labor and management. As a result, he argues, there is a serious danger of the distinctive interests of labor remaining unarticulated and inadequately
catered for. In these circumstances discontent and grievances are
liable to mount up unnoticed to the point where they constitute a
formidable threat to the whole system.

The very design of shop councils tends to alienate this institution from those whose interests it is supposed to serve....
The representatives of labor get entangled with the tasks, decisions, and - at least indirectly - interests of management....
It seems that this kind of perverted conflict regulation will increase rather than diminish both the violence and the intensity
of conflict by simultaneously opening and blocking one of its
channels of expression.

In England and the United States shop stewards ... are ...
delegates of the comprehensive interest group of labor within
the enterprise. As such ... they serve to decrease [the violence
of class conflict] ... The shop councilor [on the other hand]
... becomes part of the ruling class of industry (1959, p.263).
These shortcomings lead Dahrendorf to make a bleak prognosis for
the future course of German labor relations.

It is certainly conceivable that the future has more intense and
violent conflicts in store. To some extent there are already
indications of such a development. I have tried to show that not
all changes introduced in order to regulate industrial conflict
are well-conceived.... It would not be surprising if these ineffective modes of regulation should lead to new and at first uncontrolled outbreaks of violence; indeed it would, from the
point of view of conflict theory, be surprising if this did not
happen (1959, p.279).
The repression of conflict is likely to lead to a 'return of indus-

trial conflict with destructive consequences for German industry';
in the shorter term its effects are likely to become evident in
'ways removed from all chance of control, such as wildcat strikes,
or the election of declared Communists to works councils, and also
political activity directed against the system as such' (1969, p.
169).

It may be noted that Dahrendorf's analysis is in large part
shared by American pluralist students of Germany. The recurring
theme in their critique is the incomplete acculturation of the
Germans to the norms of democratic - viz. liberal interest group -
politics, in particular to the untidiness of its give and take,
compromises, and bargaining. Spiro (1962, p.523) has called attention to the Germans' 'desire to avoid friction by the old method
of substituting adjudication or administration for politics.'
Almond and Verba (1965, p.362) noted a tendency for their German
respondents to appear 'more at ease [with] administration rather
than politics.' This line of analysis has been more fully developed
by Edinger (1968). He reports that opinion studies have shown that:
  West Germans have not yet become accustomed to the politics of
  pluralism and that the maintenance of political stability is
  viewed largely as a function of state control rather than of
  voluntary group compromise. Not only is there a widespread in-
  clination to look on political bargaining as a nasty and sordid
  business demeaning to the state, but political controversy is
  viewed as unnecessary because the impartial state should regulate
  and arbitrate (pp.95-6).
    [Germans prefer] traditional images of the statesman and
  public servant, who are expected to be 'above' politics, a satis-
  fying answer to the clash of competing interests - which is, in
  fact, a characteristic of politics in pluralist society - but
  these images conflict with the prevalent desire for stability
  and harmony in the state (p.99).
Of course, the consequences foreseen by Dahrendorf have not
materialized in the quarter-century since the German edition of
'Class and Class Conflict.' German labor relations are still exceptional for their harmony; and German economy and society have
weathered recent international storms more successfully than many
other mature liberal democracies. Although Germany did not escape
the strike wave experienced by most European countries at the end
of the 1960s, (7) the lingering effects seem milder than elsewhere.
In short, German institutions have obviously proved less brittle
than their critics feared.

In the light of the German experience then it may not be prema-
ture to re-appraise some of the axioms of the pluralist theories of
social order. In particular, is conflict best regulated by accom-
modations between autonomous parties? In the following chapters the
proposition will be examined that in some circumstances unrestrained
group conflict may not find its own level or reach a stable resting
place but rather may lead to a spiral of disorder.

British collectivism and industrial order: Beer

In a magisterial study, Beer (1969; see also 1958 and 1973) has
described the rise of collectivist politics - or the 'new group
politics' - in Britain. Under collectivism, political decisions
are arrived at by a process of bargaining between the state and
organized interest groups. In fact, in this system the state has
increasingly come to resemble just another interest group, primus
inter pares no doubt, negotiating with other organizations - e.g.
the TUC or the CBI - for the acceptance of its policies.

The structural basis of the new group politics in Britain is the
high degree of organization of economic interests. In comparison
with the US, almost 'without exception the big vocational pressure
groups in Britain have a higher index of density and concentration'
(1958). As a result, a situation has come about where large numbers
of Britons participate, albeit indirectly and at several removes, in
a parallel system of representation based on occupation and economic
interest - a system, in Beer's terminology, of 'functional representation' or 'quasi-corporatism.' And although in theory parlia-
ment's sovereignty remains intact, 'in fact, bargaining with major
producer groups may at times lead to a kind of extra-parliamentary
legislation' (1969, p.389).

In Beer's view, the growth of collectivism is the necessary
corollary of the state's new responsibility for managing the
economy. 'The welfare state and especially the managed economy of
recent decades simply could not operate without the advice and cooperation of the great organized producer groups of business, labor,
and agriculture' (1969, p.395). Ironically, it is 'because government attempted to control or manage the economy that producer groups
acquired power to influence policy' (ibid., p.319). For, as government assumes responsibility for the economy, it finds that it must
have access to or control over the instrumentalities that are in the
command of producers and in a free country this means that it must
obtain the consent and cooperation of the groups being regulated
(ibid., p.321).

Nevertheless, and this point is central to Beer's thesis, the new
group politics would not have taken root in Britain had British
political culture not already been congenial to collectivism. 'The
easy acceptance of group representation in the present century was
facilitated by attitudes favorable to pluralism and functional representation that had survived from a much earlier time' (ibid.,
p.xii). In the post-war years, a system of political values and
beliefs that legitimated functional representation by concentrated
producers' organizations has enjoyed wide acceptance in the community and by both major political parties (ibid., pp.388,404). This is
evident, for example, in the view that 'organized groups have a
"right" to take part in making policy related to their area of
activity' (ibid., pp.329-30).

At least in his earlier writings, Beer appears to regard the
growth of collectivism as essentially a benign development. In the
epilogue to the 1969 edition of his work, however, while he still
equates the growth of collectivism with 'the process of rationalization,' Beer is pondering the irony of 'how a higher and higher
effort of rationalization can produce more and more irrationalities'

(ibid., p.409). In particular, he is ready to place some of the
blame for Britain's economic failure on the new group politics
(ibid., p.408).

One of the conspicuous failures of collectivist politics in the
management of the economy has been its inability to hold down inflation.

> Bargaining with relevant producer groups ... has not yet suc-
> ceeded in winning the co-operation necessary for an incomes
> policy that could successfully restrain these inflationary
> forces. Yet without a considerable degree of such voluntary co-
> operation, the appropriate economic policy cannot be effective
> (ibid., p.408).

Why has a viable incomes policy been beyond the reach of the new
group politics? The answer is not that it has proved impossible to
strike a bargain with the trade union movement: British unions have
in fact agreed to support wage restraint in 1948, 1964 and 1974-75.
Incomes policy failed rather because the unions were unable to
deliver the support of their members. As Beer has noted of the
TUC:

> Repeatedly its leaders have shown their inability to speak with
> authority for British labor. Nor has the fault lain solely with
> the TUC. Individual unions have also shown themselves to be im-
> potent in the face of militant action based on occupational and
> local segments of their memberships (1973, p.x).

By and large the leadership of British labor has been a force for
moderation and has supported incomes policy so long as rank and file
pressures have permitted. The case of one union leader is not un-
typical:

> 'I can't afford to lose my credibility with the people on the
> shop floor,' he said in the interview. 'That does no one any
> good - certainly not the members, not the union as an institu-
> tion, not the Labor Government.'
>
>   So Mr Basnett joined today with his colleagues in rejecting
> [the government's pay] guidelines. But at the same time, he is
> known to believe that the social contract is his members' best
> hope to have a real impact on government management of the
> economy on a day-to-day basis with their union influencing de-
> cisions on wages and prices and jobs. (8)

In other words, as Blank (1979, p.83) has pointed out, 'the
crisis in labor-government relations in the late 1960s and early
1970s *was really a crisis within the unions,* a struggle for power
between the center and the shop floor and the local unions' (emphasis added). The government and organized interest groups went on
making their bargains throughout this period but these bargains had
little or no force on the shop floor.

It would appear, then, that in his admiration for the towering
edifice of British collectivism Beer forgot to inspect its foundations. How has it come about that the 'great functional organizations of the modern economy' are 'often not masters in their own
houses' (Beer, 1969, p.423). In particular, what accounts for the
estrangement of the leadership of British labor from its rank and
file? After all, as we have seen, at the heart of Beer's argument
is the point that British political culture is especially congenial
to the new group politics. In that case, why cannot the unions,

acting in their collectivist capacity, count on the support of their members?

One possible explanation for the failure of incomes policy, then, is that support for the new group politics was not as solidly based as Beer has portrayed it. But the evidence does not support this explanation. The fact is, as Moran (1977, p.164) has pointed out, that 'voluntary incomes policies have ... generally failed though there is widespread popular support for wage restraint.' The findings of surveys and opinion polls on incomes policy have lured social scientists - not to mention politicians - into rash estimates of its viability. For example, on the eve of the miners' strike that put Britain on a three-day work-week, wrecked the Conservative government's pay policy, led to the fall of that government, and sent inflation up to close to 30 per cent, two social scientists concluded on the basis of a national sample survey that 'the prospects for an incomes policy in Britain at this time seem very much more optimistic than many prophets of doom would have us believe.' (9)

If incomes policy has enjoyed broad popular support, why has it failed repeatedly? This raises in a different form the question already posed in this chapter: how do we reconcile the apparent lack of militancy of British labor with the disorder in British industry? At every level, labor sees itself as moderate and the other levels as militant: a large proportion of the rank and file considers that the activities of 'the unions' are damaging the economy; and union leaders are constantly being forced into a more militant posture in order to pre-empt shopfloor revolts. It follows that the crisis of the new group politics cannot be satisfactorily explained by the beliefs or attitudes of British labor; in this study I argue instead that in Britain the structural preconditions of collectivism do not exist.

A Marxian account of industrial disorder: Panitch

In the 'Communist Manifesto' Marx and Engels described how 'the collisions between individual workmen and bourgeois take more and more the character of collisions between two classes.' Can Britain's industrial disorder be understood as a form of incipient class conflict?

In view of the attitudes of British workers already cited in these pages, it is not surprising that few students of British industrial relations make any such strong claim. One exception is Panitch (1976, 1979) who describes the disorder as 'the industrial expression of class conflict.' In Panitch's view, the wage claims originating on the shop floor reflect, among other things, an underlying 'dissatisfaction with existing social relations' (1976, p. 253); the opposition to the Heath Government's attempt to reform British industrial relations (the Industrial Relations Act) was a case of 'the working class united against the operation of laws that contradict the freedoms of unions as voluntary organizations' (ibid., p.249); and rank and file resistance to incomes policy arose from 'the absence of effective union input in economic decision-making and ... the absence of extensive price and profit controls and a redistributive fiscal policy' (1979, p.139).

At root, then, the actions by British workers which lead to industrial disorder are politically motivated; that is to say, they
represent challenges to the established social order and/or collective actions by the working class to protect its interests from
encroachments or threats by government. If it is true that 'this
militancy retains a non-political veneer,' that is because 'it
arises from separate segments of the working class at different
times, and arises moreover in the absence of a generalized and
explicit rejection of the economic and political structures in which
these social relations are embedded' (1976, p.253). A central argument of Panitch's (1976) book is that working-class militancy must
remain inarticulate and inchoate (i.e., limited to the industrial
arena) so long as the union movement retains its ties to a British
Labour Party dominated by an integrative, national (as opposed to
class) ideology.

The focus of Panitch's attention is the post-war relations between British unions and the Labour Party, and as a result his
treatment of shopfloor events and attitudes is perfunctory. Apart
from a partial and generally one-sided sampling of surveys and
opinion polls, Panitch produces no evidence to support the claims
he makes concerning workers' subjective motivations for undertaking
the actions that create disorder, undermine incomes policy, and
frustrate attempts to reform British industrial relations.

In fact, as we have seen, it is highly questionable whether
British workers view their actions in the way that Panitch describes. (10) However, before we can conclusively reject his
account, we must provide an alternative explanation of why British
workers engage in behavior that produces disorder; that is what the
following chapters try to do.

RECAPITULATION: VALUES AND BEHAVIOR

In the light of the preceding discussion it is possible to specify
one of the principal theoretical concerns of this study. Any attempt to understand the breakdown of order in British industry must
take account of the discrepancy between the values or attitudes and
the behavior of British labor. Values are, of course, predispo-
sitions to act in certain ways; that is, they indicate how people
will act if circumstances allow. Therefore, a discrepancy between
values and behavior should alert us to the operation of powerful
structural influences that severely limit the range of possible
actions open to people. And the contention of this study, to be
examined in the following chapters, is that the disorder in British
industry is the outgrowth of structural features of the British
system of labor relations. But before turning to the theoretical
core of the argument presented in this study, it is worth briefly
considering a competing set of explanations of the attitudes/
behavior gap.

The phenomenon has been noted by Parkin (1972, p.93) in the following terms: 'There is little evidence that workers are opposed to
trade union action in furtherance of their own particular demands,
whatever they may say in answer to questions about trade unionism in
general.' In order to account for this discrepancy, a number of
commentators have drawn a distinction between the abstract beliefs

of British workers and the beliefs governing their everyday relations with their superiors. For example, Hyman and Brough (1975,
p.62) argue that 'the acceptance of the prevailing values in their
general and abstract form ... does not preclude attitudes and actions in relation to concrete and specific issues which create
conflict and instability.' The distinction is especially clear in
Cousins's (1972) remark concerning shipyard workers' 'two separate
systems of understanding.' And in his secondary analysis of survey
data on workers' attitudes, Mann (1970, p.429) notes that 'again
there seems to be a disjunction between general abstract values and
concrete experience.' By way of illustration, Mann cites Goldthorpe
et al.'s findings that while 67 per cent of their manual sample had
seen labor-management relations in harmonistic terms, when ques-
tioned on a concrete aspect of the relationship, 55 per cent saw
work study engineers as opposed to workers' interests. I will
return to this example presently.

The drift of this line of analysis is not hard to discern, even
if it is not always spelled out in these studies. The interpretation that is being proposed is that there is a dissonance between
the dominant value system internalized by British workers, on the
one hand, and the workers' actual first-hand experience of the op-
pressiveness and irrationalities of the capitalist organization of
production, on the other. As a consequence, in Hyman and Brough's
(1975, p.211) words: 'The persistence of conflict between the
generalized value system and particular experiences and actions
opens the possibility of radicalization of ideology.' On this
interpretation, then, the contradiction is not so much between attitudes and behavior, but between abstract values and concrete expectations. The implication is left, moreover, that the abstract
values represent false consciousness, while the concrete expectations reflect the direct apprehension by the worker of the true
nature of the capitalist relations of production - at least insofar
as they touch him and his immediate fellow workers. These scattered
insights contain the germ of a truly revolutionary working-class
consciousness; but first they must be generalized and systematized
into a coherent critique of society.

This interpretation is not really susceptible of empirical falsi-
fication if it is asserted that the norms that govern concrete
everyday relations are inarticulate. At a minimum it must be
claimed that there is a gradient in workers' attitudes with the more
abstract values favorable to the existing order, and so on. This
claim is in fact made by Mann (1970, p.429): he says that 'deviant
values are more likely to be endorsed if they are presented as relevant to respondents' everyday lives.' However, the evidence does
not appear to bear out this assertion. (11) Consider Mann's example
from Goldthorpe et al. which was referred to earlier. In that
example, a majority of workers saw labor-management relations in
harmonistic terms (abstract value) but a slightly smaller majority
saw work study engineers as opposed to workers' interests (concrete
experience). However, Mann overlooks another finding reported by
Goldthorpe et al., viz., that 86 per cent of the sample said they
got on 'very well' or 'pretty well' with their foremen (1968, p.65).
In other words, workers had good relations with those situated immediately above them in the authority structure and saw a group of
staff employees - i.e., with no formal authority over them - as

inimical to their interests. As for work study engineers, we shall
look at their place in British industry in a later chapter; for the
moment let it suffice to point out that they are in an institution-
alized adversary relationship with the worker.

Accordingly, the problem of the discrepancy between the values
and the behavior of British workers does not appear to be resolved
by postulating a conflict between abstract and concrete values.

A STRUCTURAL EXPLANATION OF INDUSTRIAL DISORDER

If the beliefs professed by British workers are sincerely held, and
if they are not simply vacuous affirmations of culturally approved
values, then why are they not more often honored in practice? I
have already indicated the general nature of the explanation that
will be offered here: it is that the structure of British labor
relations creates pressures that constrain workers to behave in ways
that are inconsistent with the norms that they accept. In other
words, there exist conditions in which acting on these beliefs would
be costly and self-defeating.

If the norms do enjoy general acceptance, how can this be so? A
number of well-known recent discussions have centered on the paradox
that a large number of individual decisions may add up to an outcome
that would have been chosen by no one. Olson (1971) has shown how
it is not in the rational self-interest of an individual to contribute to the provision of a 'collective good' - i.e., one that
accrues to everyone regardless of whether they have paid for it.
Hardin (1968) has argued that commons will tend to be overgrazed:
while everyone would benefit from the upkeep of the common, no one
has any reason to look after it himself, so there develops the
tendency to overgraze it before others can complete its ruin.
Schelling (1974) has described how individual choices, each made
separately and thereby necessarily without taking account of the
interaction between them, may combine to produce a worse result for
the individuals involved than could have been obtained by coordinating those choices to take account of their mutual interaction.

The fact that some outcome is in the common interest of a large
group does not automatically give rise to the collective action
necessary to achieve it. Olson puts this point as follows:

> It is often assumed ... [that] if there is a high degree of
> agreement on what is wanted and how to get it there will almost
> certainly be effective group action. The degree of consensus is
> sometimes discussed as though it were the *only* important determi-
> nant of group action or group cohesion. There is, of course, no
> question that a lack of consensus is inimical to the prospects
> for group action.... But it does not follow that perfect con-
> sensus ... will always bring about the achievement of the group
> goal (1965, p.59).

Therefore a collective interest will not be realized unless there
exist 'selective incentives' - private benefits - that can induce
individuals to participate in providing the collective good. In
discussing ways of limiting overpopulation, Hardin makes an analo-
gous argument. To rely on appeals to conscience, he says, will be
self-defeating. For one thing, it will sooner or later be realized

that the entire cost of self-restraint is being borne by those with a conscience. Accordingly if population is to be limited there is a need for 'social arrangements that produce responsibility;' and such arrangements are likely to take the form of 'mutual coercion, mutually agreed upon.' Finally, Schelling says that if a collective good is to be realized 'what we need ... is an enforceable social contract.'

However, it should be noted that Olson's model, if not the other two, departs in one important respect from the situation described in this chapter. His model presupposes a 'rational, self-interested' actor (1965, p.2). Consequently it might explain why the purely instrumental worker does not voluntarily comply with the norms of British labor relations although he recognizes that the common interest would be served if they were generally observed; but I have argued that the British worker feels a degree of moral commitment to those norms. According to Olson, a moral code may serve as a selective incentive if it creates a sense of guilt in those who fail to contribute to the provision of the group good (ibid., p.61, footnote). In that case, why has the moral commitment not produced the necessary restraint?

The answer is that the Olson effect is likely to hold even in situations where there is a general moral consensus. Unless some government exists to impose the terms of the consensus on recalcitrants, the consensus is liable to lose its hold over the behavior of even those who are disposed to comply. For as Schelling points out:

> people who are willing to do their part as long as everybody else does, living by a commonly shared golden rule, enjoying perhaps the sheer participation in a common preference for selflessness, may have a limited tolerance to the evidence or to the mere suspicion that others are cheating on the social contract, bending the golden rule, making fools of those who carefully minimize the detergent they send into the local river or who tediously carry away the leaves they could so easily have burned (1974, p.31).

This view, it may be noted, contrasts sharply with a neo-Durkheimian one. For example, Parsons (1968, p.97, footnote 1) makes sweeping claims for the efficacy of moral consensus in preserving social order: thus he asserts that 'most societies would not dissolve into chaos on the breakdown of government.' In this study the opposite case will be argued: namely that a moral consensus will be impotent unless it is supported by effective government, that is to say, by some centralized authority invested with certain powers of coercion to enforce the consensus.

CONCLUSION

The following study, then, is an examination of the hypothesis that industrial disorder may result from the breakdown of government in the workplace - particularly within labor itself - rather than from a breakdown of value consensus. The study also examines the hypothesis that, in the British case, the breakdown of government in the workplace is a consequence of the structure of British labor relations. In order to test these hypotheses, the way in which

labor relations were conducted was studied in two closely similar
factories, one of which was in England and the other in Germany.
The site is more fully described in the next chapter.

Another concern of this study has been to trace the implications
of industrial disorder, not only for the immediate participants, but
for the national economy. Accordingly, I will also present findings
regarding the impact of disorder on the English factory's productivity. In this way I will try to indicate how Britain's relative
economic decline may be related to its form of industrial government.

Chapter 2

RESEARCH SITE AND DESIGN

What research program was adopted in order to answer the questions raised in chapter 1? In this chapter I outline the considerations that influenced the choice of the study's research site and design; I briefly describe the research settings; and I give an account of the research methods employed.

CHOICE OF RESEARCH SITE AND DESIGN

In chapter 1 we looked at the reason for rejecting explanations of the industrial disorder in Britain that postulated a breakdown in value consensus; instead, it was suggested, this disorder is the outcome of a breakdown of government in the workplace. The approach that was adopted in order to test this hypothesis was a comparative case-study of two factories of an international corporation engaged in the manufacture of tires. One of these factories is in England, the other is in Germany.

The decision to make the factory the unit of analysis - and, within the factory, largely a single department - was dictated by the nature of the phenomenon under investigation. We shall see that it is very difficult to obtain satisfactory statistical measures for the incidence of what the Donovan Commission called the 'disorder in factory and workshop relations' in Britain. This disorder does not consist of a finite number of discrete events like work stoppages; rather, it takes the form of endemic friction in everyday relations on the shop floor. The research instrument employed, then, had to be sensitive enough to permit the analysis of numerous small-scale interactions in the workplace. Accordingly, I chose to conduct an intensive observation of the same department in two matched factories.

This in-depth analysis was possible, of course, only at the expense of greater breadth of coverage. In order to offset this limitation, I have taken some pains to indicate the respects in which my two cases are and are not representative by reference to the literature on each country's labor relations; this has entailed the extensive footnoting of relevant case-studies, surveys, statutes, government reports, and so on, for which the reader's indulgence is asked in advance.

By selecting an international corporation making the same product, I hoped to locate two closely matched factories. My object was to find an approximation to a natural experiment in order to isolate the effects on workplace relations of each country's system of labor relations. Obviously British and German industry differ in a number of other ways that may affect the level of industrial order in each country. In this study I wanted to focus on the consequences of differences in the two countries' national labor relations systems. Hence I chose a setting where other differences were eliminated or minimally present. In the event, of course, some extraneous differences did remain, and later in this chapter I attempt to estimate whether or not they may have influenced workplace relations.

It is worth pointing out an important consequence of this research design: it is that the two factories do not represent modal instances of the universe of British and German factories; nor are they intended to do so. It is precisely because these factories are alike (and therefore probably unrepresentative of their respective countries) that they present an exceptional opportunity for evaluating the effects of differences in the structure of labor relations in each country.

Why pair and English and a German factory? In addition to Germany's reputation for industrial order a number of other considerations influenced this choice. Panic (1976) has pointed out that the United Kingdom and West Germany are similar with respect to size, endowment in natural resources, the stage of industrial development reached and dependence on foreign trade. Panic also found that the industrial structure (1) of the two countries is very similar; and it was even more so in 1972 than in the mid-1950s. In spite of these similarities, there was not a single major branch of industrial activity in which the UK performed better over the period 1958-72. Panic's analysis would suggest that Germany's superior economic performance in the post-war years may be explained by social and political rather than by economic factors.

THE FACTORIES

In the following sections the factories are briefly compared in terms of physical characteristics, workers and managers. The intention is not simply to set the stage for the discussion that follows but to identify possible competing sources for the variations in workplace behavior.

Physical characteristics of the factories

The two factories presented a number of contrasts - in terms of age, size, and range of products. The English factory had been started up between the wars and enjoyed something of a flagship status among the firm's plants. Over the years existing buildings had been extended and new buildings added. Consequently the factory was made up of several independent structures of different ages, some of them two-storied. In contrast, the German factory had been constructed

all of a piece in the 1960s; it consisted of one building on a
single level. There was no sign that the age of the bricks and
mortar in either factory affected operations there; however, the
differences of layout had obvious consequences for the coordination
of production. At certain points in the English factory materials
or components had to be transferred between operations by a conveyor
system of internal transport; in Germany such a need did not arise
since operations were located in sequence on the factory floor.

The English factory was much larger than the German - it had
three times the total floor space - and it manufactured a more diversified range of products. Although both factories produced certain staples - passenger, truck, and rear tractor tires - only the
English factory still made crossply and fabric radial models in addition to steel radials. (2) Again it seems clear that the greater
diversity of models and types manufactured in the English factory
complicated production scheduling there.

A further difference may have affected operations in the two
factories. Shortly after the oil price rises in 1974 the German
factory's operations had been run down and over half the workforce
had been made redundant. For a while the company appears to have
been contemplating closing the factory down. The workforce had been
steadily rebuilt since then, but it was still far short of the
plant's physical capacity. By contrast, so far as the untrained eye
could judge, the English factory was overcrowded. As a result the
aisles of the English factory were often obstructed and trucks of
components became snarled in traffic jams in the storage areas; in
Germany materials and components were stored in well-ordered rows,
often adjacent to the operations where they were next to be used.
It is quite probable that the congestion in the English factory
weakened management's control over production (e.g., by making accurate quantity checks next to impossible), with consequences that
will be examined in later chapters.

The English factory's workforce was over six times the size of
the German. A growing body of evidence tends to implicate factory
size in loss of managerial control, in Britain at least. (3) It
cannot be ruled out, then, that the size-difference contributed to
the contrasts between the two factories' labor relations' climates.

In view of the higher costs of labor in Germany, one might have
expected to find a greater investment in capital equipment in the
German factory. In fact, virtually identical machinery and production techniques were employed in each factory (after allowance is
made for the greater range of tires produced in England). There
appear to be at least two reasons for this. First, since the company was manufacturing a highly visible product for the world market,
it had to maintain consistent quality standards throughout its
plants. This meant using the same standard of equipment regardless
of local economic advantages of substituting labor for capital. In
fact, the standardization of equipment occasionally exasperated
local management: the German factory was obliged to use a make of
force variation machine to test its tires that was different from
the one used by its customers. As a result the customers sometimes
rejected tires that the factory had approved. The second reason why
similar equipment was in use in each factory may have been the fact
that it was largely of company make (e.g., the tirebuilding ma-

chines) or built according to company specifications. Obviously,
the longer the production run, the more quickly the costs of design-
ing and manufacturing the equipment can be amortized. (4)

   In any case, for the present it is necessary only to note that
each factory used the same or similar equipment and production techniques. Therefore the differing systems of workplace relations in
the two factories cannot be the outcome of differing technological
conditions. (5) This point is important because the technology of
tire production has been singled out as one that is particularly
congenial to fractional bargaining - that is, dispersed bargaining
conducted by separate work groups either outside or in conflict with
the formal procedures. (6) In this case the technology of tire
production may explain the absolute level of fractional bargaining
in the two plants; but it cannot account for any difference between
them.

The workers

No survey was made of the factories' workforces, but information
drawn from the personnel records makes it possible to highlight some
of the more important differences and similarities. (7) My remarks
will be restricted to the production workers since they formed the
principal focus of the field work.

   The English workforce was on average substantially older than the
German and had considerably greater length of service. (8) These
differences are partly accounted for by the different ages of the
factories, but they also reflect the German factory's higher rate
of labor turnover. In the two years preceding the field work the
crude separation rates - i.e., numbers of leavers in the year as a
proportion of the total workforce - had been running at 5 per cent
in the English factory and at 33 per cent in the German factory.
This large disparity probably resulted from a number of circumstances. First, the German labor market provided greater opportunity for changing employment. Over the previous five years the
rate of unemployment in Germany had averaged about half the English
rate. (9) Immediately preceding the oil crisis, i.e. in 1973, separations in the English factory had been 16 per cent. Second, the
German factory had been rebuilding its workforce after the mass redundancies of three years earlier. The relevance of this point is
that, in both factories, recent hires predominated among the
leavers. For example, the attrition rate among trainee tirebuilders was particularly high. Of the learners listed on the
German labor line-up one year before my visit only 30 per cent remained. (Some of these may have been transferred to other departments.) Eighty per cent of the English tirebuilders who had quit
in the 9 months preceding the fieldwork had less than one year's
service with the company. Since the German workforce was being ex-
panded it contained a larger proportion of new recruits whose greater propensity to quit inflated the labor turnover rate. Third, the
German workforce was younger; age of workforce tends to be nega-
tively related to labor turnover. However, the higher labor turnover rate is apparently also a reflection of management's greater
freedom to dismiss workers in the German factory. One half of the

German separations were dismissals, compared to only one tenth of
the English.   In at least two thirds of the German dismissals the
consent of the works council had been required by law. (10)
    A substantial proportion of each workforce was foreign-born.   Im-
migrants from the Indian subcontinent and the West Indies accounted
for approximately 30 per cent of the English factory's production
workforce;   and one of every two production workers in the German
factory was a guest worker (11) - in this case usually a Turk or a
Yugoslav.   An important difference between the situation of the
guest worker in Germany and that of the immigrant in Britain should
be noted.   The immigrant to Britain is usually permanently settled
and his status is indistinguishable from that of the indigenous
workers.   The guest worker, on the other hand, is (in theory at
least) only a visitor.   He has a temporary residence permit, normally renewable annually.   If he loses his job, he is entitled to collect unemployment benefits for one year;   if he is still unemployed
at the end of that time, his residence permit is not renewed.
    It would be wrong to overstate the contrast.   After five years
the guest worker becomes entitled to a permanent residence permit;
and after ten years he may petition for naturalization.   In practice
it has turned out that after a prolonged stay foreign workers increasingly wish to live permanently in Germany and have their families join them there.   Nevertheless, on the evidence of Mehrländer's
(1974) survey, it would appear that most guest workers retain the
intention of returning to their home countries.   According to a
Turkish works councillor in the German factory, no more than 10 per
cent of the Turkish workers planned to remain in Germany.   When it
comes to understanding their behavior, it is probably the foreign
workers' intentions that are most helpful.   How did the presence of
these foreign workers affect the two factories' labor relations?
And what were the effects - if any - of their differing situations
in England and Germany?
    In both cases the foreign workers were in general more industri-
ous than the natives.   For example, in one month guest workers accounted for all but 2 per cent of the overtime worked by tirebuilders, although they made up only 60 per cent of their number.
For the same month the earnings of Yugoslav tirebuilders were 13 per
cent above the Germans' even after making allowance for overtime.
The same pattern was evident in the English tire room.   There the
tirebuilders were operating an overtime ban, but among the servicemen - whose job it was to deliver components to the builders - those
with Indian and Pakistani names worked an average of 16 hours' overtime (in the course of a week for which the records were examined).
One of them had worked a 77-hour week.   During the same week the
other servicemen (some of whom were West Indians) worked an average
of 4½ hours' overtime.
    In both factories foreign workers tended to be overrepresented in
the dirty, menial, and lower-paid jobs. (12)   (In Germany the Yugoslavs fared better than the Turks.)   In the English tire room Asians
were greatly overrepresented among the servicemen.   (In fact every
eighth serviceman was called Singh.)   These servicemen were markedly
worse off than their (predominantly Turkish) counterparts in
Germany.   According to my calculations their earnings, exclusive of
overtime, averaged 75 per cent of the tirebuilders' earnings;   in
the German factory the corresponding figure was 89 per cent.

The longer-term orientation of the immigrant workers might have been expected to lead them to resort to collective action, if necessary, to stake out their claim in the English factory. Conversely, the shorter time-frame of the guest workers, as well as their more precarious situation in their host country, might have been expected to discourage any such action. Indeed, Mehrländer's survey shows that they tend to have a predominantly instrumental and individualistic approach to their work. Can the contrasting labor relations climate in the two factories (to be described in the remaining chapters) be accounted for in part by the different situations of their foreign workers? On the evidence of the present study, the answer is no. Neither expectation was borne out. In the English factory the immigrant workers stayed very much in the background in the endemic fractional bargaining. For example, in spite of the large disparity between their earnings, the (predominantly Asian) servicemen were conspicuously less aggressive in pursuing their demands than the tirebuilders. And in Germany, as I shall show in chapter 4, the closest brushes with fractional bargaining involved Turkish workers. While there is little systematic evidence available, this pattern appears to be consistent with the national experience in Britain and Germany. Immigrant workers have rarely been in the forefront of industrial unrest in Britain. (13) By contrast, in Germany guest workers were especially prominent in the 1973 wave of wildcat strikes (e.g., in the so-called Türkenstreik at Ford), although their part in the September strikes in 1969 had been relatively small. The contrast between the two factories, then, cannot be explained away as an artifact of the different situations of the foreign workers.

In passing it should be noted that the fact that a large proportion of each production workforce was foreign strengthens the case for looking for the structural determinants of order and disorder in the workplace. If such stereotypically German traits as orderliness and industry are displayed by a workforce that is half made up of foreigners, then they can no longer be convincingly explained as the outcome of the fabled native diligence of the German worker. Rather, this study tries to show, these traits result from the social organization of the German factory.

In neither case had production workers received any formal training in the skills required in tire manufacture. Although many of the operations were highly skilled all training had to be provided within the factory; because the industry is a small one and the necessary skills are highly specific there is no labor market for rubber workers as such.

Absenteeism was very much higher in the German factory. It was not possible to make a direct comparison because records were not maintained on the same basis. In England the rate of absenteeism from all causes averaged 5 per cent; in Germany the rate from sickness alone (for all employees, not just production workers) was 6.15 per cent. It is probable that the higher German rate was at least in part due to the more generous sickness benefits that the law imposes on German employers. In case of sickness a German worker was guaranteed full earnings for the first six weeks; in England sickness entailed a substantial loss of earnings. (14)

Finally, it should be mentioned that the English factory was

situated in a large conurbation while the German factory was in a
small town. As Slichter et al. (1960, p.519) report, there is evidence that smaller and more rural communities tend to have a climate
favorable to high worker efficiency, superior union-management relations and cooperative employee attitudes. (15)

Management

The close control exercised by the parent corporation had resulted
in very similar managerial styles and policies in the two factories.
This control was felt in a number of different ways. First, decision-making over a broad range of issues was retained by the
parent company. Second, certain key management positions in both
factories were filled by parent company personnel. Third, the
factories' organizational structure and operating procedures were
prescribed by the parent company. Fourth, the factories' operations
were constantly monitored by staff on visits from the parent company. And finally, local management had been recreated in the
parent's image by the application of uniform policies regarding
personnel selection, training and promotion.

Before I look at these points in greater detail, it is worth
quoting from an earlier description of the relationship between the
parent company and its British subsidiary. The author of this description (16) had identified three types of parent-subsidiary relations. The company that is the subject of this study was cited
as an example of one of those types.

[This type of] relationship implies that both the organization
and internal administration of the British firm follow very
closely along the lines of the [parent company], and that either
top-ranking managerial executives are [parent] nationals, or the
whole approach to decision-taking is directed along [parent com-
pany] lines. It also suggests that all decisions of any importance - apart from those associated with the day-to-day operation of the plant - and their means of implementation, have to be
referred back for approval to the [parent company], e.g., in respect of such matters as finance and capital expenditures,
changes in product range or design, prices and profit margins,
production methods, sales estimates and sales budgets, advertis-
ing policy and recruitment of senior staff. In addition, copies
of all Board Meeting minutes, regular statements - sometimes
daily, but usually weekly - relating to production, finance and
sales, have to be dispatched to the [parent company].... As a
matter of principle both ... manufacturing techniques and managerial methods, such as those relating to production, purchasing,
personnel, [etc.] are (consciously) assimilated and rigidly adhered to wherever possible. Very frequent interchanges of personnel take place between [parent] and U.K. plants, management,
production, costing, time and motion experts paying special
visits wherever a change in departmental policy in [the parent
company] needs to be implemented in the branch plant. Export
orders are often routed by the parent company and integrated with
its own and other overseas subsidiaries' production capacity.
Under this type of control, the U.K. branch tends to be simply a

duplicate, or mouthpiece, of the parent company, having little
freedom of autonomy of its own. Some [parent companies] provide
their subsidiaries with the most detailed operating manuals,
which are regularly brought up-to-date and revised. More often
than not, all fundamental research and development is centralized in the [parent company] and only a limited amount of applied
research is carried out by the subsidiary.

It should not be imagined that this account was describing a
transitional arrangement; at the time it was written the English
subsidiary had already been in existence for over a quarter-century.
In its essentials this account still held - and for both subsidiaries - at the time of my field work. The following remarks bring
the account up to date by briefly reviewing the degree and nature of
the parental control exercised over both factories.

As would be expected, the power to make policy decisions - e.g.,
finance, product lines, introduction of new equipment - remained
entirely in parent company hands; but the writ of the parent company ran to a surprising extent on the shop floor itself. This was
most conspicuously the case when it came to production methods and
technical standards. It appeared that even relatively minor specification changes had to receive prior parent company approval.
However, other less technical aspects of management were also subject to detailed central control. For example, there were constant
interplant comparisons of manning, productivity and quality aimed at
generalizing best practice. It goes without saying that financial
and production statistics were prepared and reported on a uniform
basis laid down by the parent company; in addition, a not incon-
siderable part of local management's time was occupied in preparing
standard returns or ad hoc reports, answering questions from the
parent, attending company-wide meetings and conferences, receiving
visits from a succession of experts, and so on.

It is true that, because of national variations, labor relations
matters were not susceptible to the same degree of centralized direction. Nonetheless even in this area the parent company insisted
on approving major decisions (e.g., how to handle a serious work
stoppage) and had reportedly involved itself in issues as detailed
as individual disciplinary cases.

In short, the parent company made its presence felt at every
level of the two factories. The prime instrument for this purpose
was a large, central staff of functional experts that conducted
R & D, served as a channel to disseminate technical standards, and
generally monitored the activities of the far-flung outposts of the
corporate empire.

While each factory's management was composed preponderantly of
local nationals, certain key positions were filled by expatriates.
Of interest for us is the fact that, in each case, the managing
director (i.e., chief executive officer) and the two most senior
production managers were parent company nationals. So too, in
England, was the manager of the technical division. It is interesting to note that the production director in the English factory
had previously served in the same capacity in the German factory.

In both factories the senior personnel manager was a local national. In addition, middle and lower management positions were
exclusively staffed by nationals. It appeared to be company policy

to fill managerial positions by internal promotion. In the English
passenger tire plant all the production managers had spent virtually
their entire working lives with the company. And although the
German factory was newer the same pattern was already establishing
itself there. Two thirds of all the production managers and supervisors had started with the factory within two years of its opening.

In terms of formal qualifications there was little to distinguish
the two managements. This point is worth underlining because other
studies suggest that there is generally a greater stress on formal
training in German industry. For example, it is apparently uncommon
in German industry for a supervisor not to possess a Meisterbrief
(foreman's certificate). (17) In the factory that I studied, however, not a single production supervisor had gone through the
arduous process of qualifying as a Meister ($3\frac{1}{2}$ years of apprentice-
ship, 2 years in a skilled trade, and 2 examinations). In the tire
room, for example, all the supervisors had started as tirebuilders
(the same was true of two thirds of the English tire room supervisors) and had been promoted from the ranks.

Above the level of supervisor it is apparently exceptional for a
German manager not to have been to Ingenieurschule. However, in
this case only a fraction had actually done so. In the English
passenger tire plant none of the production managers had a university degree.

It appeared to be a fairly common practice for local managers to
be temporarily assigned (for 2- to 6-month spells) to the parent
company in order to learn about new technical developments and/or
for the purpose of general indoctrination. Actual foreign postings
were much less common, but not unknown. For instance, the production control manager in the English passenger tire plant, an
Englishman, had recently spent four years in the German factory
where he had designed, installed and run the production control
system that he was operating in England. There were frequent short-
term visits and contacts, even at relatively junior levels.

From Figure 2.1 it will be seen that the organizational structure
of management followed broadly the same outline in each factory. No
doubt this sort of isomorphism is to be expected where a parent company exercises detailed control over the operations of the subsidiaries;   communication is obviously facilitated if each parent company specialty has opposite numbers in the subsidiaries. One structural difference between the factories may be noted: the supervisory span of control was much greater in the German factory (the
ratio of first-line supervision to production workers was 1:22 as
compared with 1:14 in the English factory). However, in Germany
some routine supervisory work was undertaken by production workers -
an arrangement that would have clashed with a union boundary in
England.

RESEARCH METHODS

The materials for this study were gathered primarily in the course
of the intensive observation of the same department - the tire room
- in each factory over a period of four weeks. (18) (For the place
of the tire room in the productive process see below.) In each case

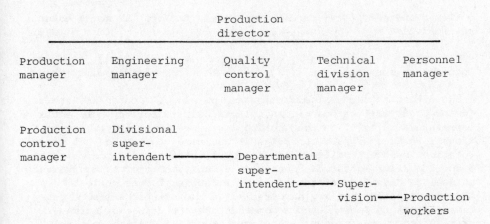

Figure 2.1 Abridged organization chart - English and German factory

Source: Organization charts for the English passenger tire plant and the German factory.

I systematically observed the activities of a sample of each group of employees - tire builders, servicemen and supervisors. Generally the observation periods lasted between two and five hours and were scheduled to cover different stages of the shift. Longer observation periods (e.g., for a full eight-hour shift) would have exhausted the patience of my subjects without materially adding to my information. Moreover, the shorter observation periods permitted a broader sample and greater flexibility in accommodating the observation to other aspects of the research. The program of observation was not adhered to rigidly, however, and not infrequently observations were interrupted or broken off if other targets of opportunity presented themselves - e.g., a delegation of workers left their machines to call on the personnel manager. In addition to the tire room one other department was observed for three days. No restrictions were placed on my freedom to move about the factories. Although I had been apprehensive about possible reactions to my constant presence on the shop floor, an initial mild curiosity quickly gave way to a gratifying indifference.

The program of observation was supplemented and supported by information from other sources.

Interviews

In each factory I interviewed every level of production management, from the tire room manager up through the chain of command to the production director; the German factory's personnel manager and the English passenger tire plant's labor relations manager; various other staff managers and labor representatives. The interviews were informal and they lasted between half an hour and four hours.

In addition to the interviews I was in almost daily contact with certain employees: personnel managers, industrial engineers; in the English factory, the tire room shop steward and the branch

chairman and secretary;   and in the German factory the works council
chairman.

Documentary sources

I had access to certain production and personnel records in each
factory. As will become evident, I was able to collect more ample
documentary material in the English factory. There are two explanations for this: first, in England I was given the run of the labor
relations manager's files; in Germany I obtained only the materials
I specifically requested. Second, the English factory's management
maintained detailed records of labor relations issues while the
German did not; this may have reflected the greater salience of
these issues in England and a somewhat greater degree of bureau-
cratization there (presumably on account of the English factory's
greater size).

Other sources

I attended a wide variety of formal and informal meetings, which it
would be tedious to enumerate. In only one case was I refused
access to a meeting - a formal session of the German works council -
although I was present at meeting between the council and management. Wherever possible the sources of my data are given in the
body of the text or by footnote.
    It is worth repeating that I did not bind myself in advance to a
detailed research format. The actual techniques adopted varied according to local circumstances and opportunities. Inevitably the
usefulness of my informants often depended less on their formal
status than on their personal character - openness, inquisitiveness
and so on. It was not unusual, moreoever, for the visits or telephone calls that interrupted interviews to be more revealing than
the interviews themselves.

THE TIRE INDUSTRY

It remains to complete the backdrop for the subsequent discussion by
describing the tire manufacturing process and the circumstances of
the tire industry in the late 1970s.

The manufacturing process

In each factory I observed the operations in the passenger tire
room. (Since the German factory produced only steel radial tires,
I concentrated on this type in the English factory as well.) What
was the place of the tire room in the manufacturing process?
    The most popular size of steel radial passenger tire contains
eight distinct components - a few of them subassemblies themselves.
Most of the components are strips of rubber (strictly, rubber and
chemical compound) of differing sizes and contours, e.g., treads,

sidewalls and chafers. The tire ply is rubberized fabric; the
steel belt or band is rubberized wire mesh; and the bead is strands
of steel wire coated with rubber and wrapped in fabric. These components are produced in various stock preparation departments for
assembly in the tire room. The assembly of the components (or tirebuilding) is done by operators (called tirebuilders) working at
separate semi-automatic machines. The tirebuilders are kept supplied with the appropriate components by servicemen; the servicemen
also remove the built (green) tires and take them to the next stage
in the process, the curing department, where they are placed in
molds for vulcanization or curing at intense heat and pressure.
Once the curing is complete the tires are trimmed, given a final
inspection, tested for internal balance on force variation machines,
and are placed in storage to await shipment out of the factory.

Even from this brief account it will be apparent that a break in
the flow of a single component can bring the operations in the tire
room to a halt. Kuhn (1961, pp.151-2) has described a number of
other distinctive characteristics of the production process. First,
a good deal of the work is performed by hand, and therefore the
output of any department is sensitive to the pace at which the
workers desire to work. Second, the process is not comparable to
an oil refining plant where machinery or the process itself deter-
mines pace and speed of output. Production in a tire factory cannot
continue unless the workers are on the job. Third, rubber stock and
finished tires are very bulky and space is ordinarily too limited or
expensive for management to produce for storage. Fourth, another
reason to avoid sizeable inventories is that mixed rubber deteri-
orates if not cured. Kuhn has noted that these characteristics of
the production process mean that a slowdown or stoppage by even a
small group of workers can have an impact on production out of proportion to the number directly involved. This presents workers with
the opportunity and the temptation to bargain fractionally.

Largely because of the nature of the production process and the
weight of the capital investment involved, each factory worked its
equipment round-the-clock. The basic pattern in each case was three
eight-hour shifts per day for five days per week. (19) Workers
rotated through the shifts on a weekly basis. Although technological changes had progressively removed the physical effort from
the work, certain tasks (tirebuilding among them) remained very
strenuous. Technology had also had the effect of altering the skill
ratios of various jobs and thus upsetting the historical relationships between them. In this process the tirebuilders were clearly
losers and the leading hands in the stock-preparation departments
(who were now responsible for increasingly sophisticated equipment)
were gainers. The newer German factory, of course, did not have to
contend with these problems to the same extent.

The world tire market

In recent years the world (and particularly the European) tire industry has been experiencing a crisis of overcapacity. One estimate
put the overcapacity in Europe and the US at 25-30 per cent in 1979.
(20)

This overcapacity is the outcome of a combination of different factors: overexpansion in the 1960s when automobile ownership was booming; imports from Eastern Europe and Japan; a reduction in driving following the oil crisis. However, the single most important factor has been the displacement of the traditional crossply tire by the radial tire, which has a life twice as long. By early 1978 steel radial tires were being fitted to four out of five new European automobiles. (21)

The result has been intense price and quality competition and a wave of plant closures and redundancies. In Britain, Goodyear has closed its Glasgow factory (22) and Dunlop its Merseyside factory; in Germany Phoenix has been forced out of the business; and Uniroyal has sold its European operations to Continental. (23) However, the British tire industry appears to have been worse hit than the German. The number of jobs in the industry declined from 47,000 in 1973 to 40,300 in 1978. (24) A British government report found that relative production efficiency needs to be increased by up to 30 per cent compared with European competition. (25) And the major British manufacturer, Dunlop, asked the British government for £46 million subsidy. (26)

It is against the background of these developments that the events reported in this study took place. It will be recalled that in 1974 the German factory had been on the point of closing; the English factory had experienced bouts of short-working and lay-offs and a small number of voluntary redundancies.

CONCLUSION

As stated in chapter 1, the aim of this study was to examine three propositions: first, that the disorder in British industry (as compared with the order in German industry) is the outcome of a breakdown of government in the workplace; second, that this breakdown is a consequence of the structure of British labor relations; and third, that this disorder is implicated in the slow rate of growth of Britain's industrial productivity.

How were the objectives of the study served by the research design described in this chapter? First, the detailed observation of of day-to-day labor relations in each factory made possible a first-hand analysis of the causes of order and disorder in each workplace. Second, the selection of two matched factories eliminated a number of possible alternative explanations for the greater disorder in the English factory. This disorder - or, strictly, the differential between the two factories - cannot be explained as the result of differences between managements, technology, or even workers, for, as we have seen, the factories were similar or identical in all these respects. That left, it is true, many other respects in which the factories were not matched; but, with few exceptions, (27) the remaining differences were not ones which are commonly associated with differences in labor relations. The research design, then, has not totally isolated the effects of the two national labor relations systems, but has succeeded in narrowing down the number of possible explanations. Third, the similarities between the two factories (especially the fact that they manufacture the same product) facilitated the productivity comparison, and the detailed observation of the factories' operations permitted me to identify the ways in which the productivity levels were affected by labor relations.

I now turn to an account of those differences in labor relations on which the research design focuses.

Chapter 3

FORMAL STRUCTURES OF WORKPLACE LABOR REPRESENTATION

INTRODUCTION

Before going on to examine the systems of labor representation in the English and German factories, it is worth reminding ourselves of the reason why the workplace has been made the focus of attention in this study. Why not have concentrated instead, for example, on the structure of organized labor in each country? After all, as Ross (1962, p.333) has observed, European unions have tended to be 'strongest at the center and weakest at the local or plant level; in fact they frequently do not have any formal existence or "presence" inside the plant.' Labor relations, as a result, has largely meant the relations between trade unions and employers' associations.

The reason for looking at the workplace is that the traditional system of industry-wide collective bargaining has been progressively undermined in the post-war years by sustained full employment and prosperity. Ross (p.331) points out that these systems became set in their present forms 'in an era of frequent unemployment, low wages and subsistence living standards. The dominant purpose was to protect workers ... against unrestricted wage cutting in the labor market.' In these conditions, European labor unions contrived to maintain earnings above their true market levels by concluding industry-wide collective agreements.

However, in the post-war years the reserve armies of the unemployed have been replaced by chronic labor shortages. In these changed circumstances the wage rates fixed by industry-wide collective bargaining have lagged behind what the market has been ready to pay. These industry agreements have been tailored to the circumstances of the marginal firms in the industry. More prosperous firms have been in a position to pay wages substantially in excess of the officially negotiated rates and, with full order books and in a tight labor market, they have had every incentive to do so. In consequence actual earnings in European countries have far outstripped negotiated wage rates. This is, of course, the phenomenon known as wage drift.

From our point of view, the most interesting consequence of this development is the effect it has had on the structure of labor rela-

tions in England and Germany. This effect has been described by
Ross as a shift in the center of gravity of European labor relations. Increasingly, 'what is said and done by employer associations is becoming less important; what goes on in plants and
localities counts for more' (op.cit., pp.336-7). For this reason,
to understand the causes of industrial disorder, it is essential to
examine how workplace labor organization in each country has reacted
to this greatly enlarged scope for the autonomous conduct of labor
relations at plant level.

WORKPLACE LABOR ORGANIZATION IN BRITAIN

In 1968 a British Royal Commission (1) reported that the central
defect of the British system of labor relations was 'the disorder in
factory and workshop relations and pay structures' (Donovan, 1968,
p.40). The roots of this problem were to be found in the breakdown
of the system of regulation by industry-wide agreements between employers' associations and trade unions and in the failure of an
alternative system, based on the workplace, to emerge in its place.
    For various reasons, foremost among them full employment, the
post-war years had seen a shift in the site of effective bargaining
to the workplace. Increasingly actual earnings were determined by
bargaining within factories and had drifted far apart from the rates
laid down in industry-wide agreements. (2) The problem was that at
this level bargaining
    is largely outside the control of employers' associations and
    trade unions. It usually takes place piecemeal and results in
    competitive sectional wage adjustments and chaotic pay struc-
    tures.... These developments help to explain why resort to un-
    official and unconstitutional strikes and other forms of workshop
    pressure has been increasing (op.cit., p.261).
Why had no orderly system for the regulation of labor relations
in the workplace filled the vacuum left by the disintegration of the
system of industry-wide regulation? Donovan placed the blame on the
tendency of both employers and unions to cling to the pretense of
industry bargaining. Union 'leaders have remained preoccupied with
collective bargaining at industry level, while shop stewards have
been left largely on their own to set the pace in negotiations at
plant level' (p.107). In the view of the report, industry bargaining had become an obstacle in the way of the reforms necessary to
restore order to British workplace relations.
    The instrument Donovan proposed for this purpose was the factory
agreement - 'an agreement which deals comprehensively with the terms
and conditions of employment for all employees at a particular establishment' (p.10). The factory agreement, unlike the unwieldy industry agreement, could come to grips with the specific irritants in
the workplace. 'Factory agreements ... can regulate actual pay,
constitute a factory negotiating committee and grievance procedures
which suit the circumstances, deal with such subjects as redundancy
and discipline and cover the rights and obligations of shop
stewards. A factory agreement can assist competent managers, many
industry-wide agreements have become a hindrance to them' (pp.
262-3).

Accordingly most of Donovan's detailed recommendations were designed to give effect to the introduction of factory agreements and
to point out the benefits they would make possible.

To the disappointment of some of its critics (3) the Donovan
Commission did not propose penalties for 'strikes in breach of obligations imposed by collective agreements.' While not in principle
opposed to the use of legal sanctions for the enforcement of agreed
procedures, Donovan felt that such a step would be counterproductive
if taken before the reform of the system itself. In the existing
circumstances it 'would divert attention from the underlying causes
to the symptoms and might indeed delay or even frustrate the cure we
recommend' (ch.9).

Donovan's analysis is the same as, or very close to, my own
almost a decade later. (4) Therefore it will be useful to examine
the structure of labor representation within the English factory in
light of the specific recommendations made in the report. To what
extent did the formal institutions of labor relations in the factory, and in particular its form of worker representation, embody the
reforms proposed by Donovan?

Shop stewards in British industry

The Donovan Commission pinned its main hope on the formalization and
the codification of the role of the shop steward. (5) Since power
had now passed irrevocably to the shop floor, any reconstruction of
British labor relations had to take place on the foundation of the
shop steward system. Hitherto 'the shop steward system had developed its strength in an informal and piecemeal way' (p.107).
Donovan therefore proposed a program of measures intended to integrate the shop steward into a new formal system for the regulation
of labor relations. In particular, the shop stewards (or a committee drawn from their number) were to negotiate the factory agreement with management. However, this would first require a reform of
the existing official institutions on both sides of industry. On
the one hand, employers would have to recognize the shop stewards as
full negotiating partners and grant them the necessary facilities to
represent the workforce; and, on the other, 'the processes of union
government should be modified to accommodate shop stewards ... more
adequately than they do now' (p.186).

It would be an oversimplification to see in Donovan's recommendations merely a strategy for domesticating the new power of shop
stewards. It is true that the reforms contemplated extending de
jure recognition to some of the powers already in their hands; and
that by making shop stewards parties to collective agreements it was
hoped that they would come to have a greater stake in their observance. But it was not so much the shop stewards' power that
alarmed Donovan, as their weakness. The report noted that 'it does
not follow ... that shop stewards and work groups exercise effective
control where industry-wide agreements and managers fail to do so
.... In [certain] circumstances industrial relations can border on
anarchy' (p.28). In a widely quoted finding, a survey commissioned
by Donovan had reported that 'for the most part the steward is
viewed by others, and views himself, as an accepted, reasonable and

even moderating influence; more of a lubricant than an irritant'
(McCarthy, 1966, p.56). Consequently it would be wrong to think of
the proposed reforms as an attempt to co-opt or buy off disturbers
of the industrial peace. They were intended, rather, to consolidate
the authority of those in the workplace who 'quite commonly ... are
supporters of order exercising a restraining influence on their
members in conditions which promote disorder' (p.29).

Labor representation in the English factory

How far had Donovan's reforms been implemented in the English factory? At the time of my field work, industry agreements were still
being negotiated for the rubber industry in Britain. However, in
accordance with Donovan's recommendations, they set only minimum
rates of pay which companies were free to exceed (p.43). Actual
rates of pay and conditions of work were negotiated at factory
level. (6) However there was no comprehensive factory agreement at
this level since each major group of unionized employees bargained
separately with the company: production workers, engineers, and
staff and supervisory employees each constituted independent collective bargaining units. (7) This marks a significant departure
from Donovan's recommendations, and its implications will be explored in a later chapter. (8)
    For all practical purposes the bargaining units were coterminous
with union boundaries within the factory. The one exception was the
engineers who were organized by two different unions (which appeared
to have worked out a harmonious modus vivendi). In all, then, four
unions had members in the factory. It is well-known that multi-
unionism is common in British industry. In this case, some of the
ills associated with it - usually arising out of inter-union competition for membership - may have been mitigated by the existence of
clear occupational spheres of interest. The situation, therefore,
approximated the principle proposed by Donovan, namely 'one union
for one grade of work within one factory.'
    In considering the detailed arrangements for the representation
of labor in the English factory, and in particular the role of the
shop steward, my remarks will be limited to the production workers.

Shop steward and union in the English factory

As noted earlier, Donovan recommended that 'the processes of union
government should be modified to accommodate shop stewards and work
groups more adequately' (p.186).
    In principle the integration of the shop steward system into the
structure of the union should have been made easier in this case by
the fact that the union branch was based on the workplace. It is
common in Britain for the union branch - 'the basic unit of union
governmental organization' (Turner et al., 1967, p.203) - to be
geographically based and to bring together workers from many different factories who happen to live in the same locality. This
practice has meant, as Donovan pointed out, that 'the branch is ...
divorced from the real business of the union at the place of work,

but it nevertheless remains the official means of contact between the union and its members' (op.cit., p.30). In this case the system of workplace labor representation - viz., the shop stewards - was formally part of the union structure. The convenor of shop stewards was at the same time chairman of the branch; he and three other senior stewards were elected plant-wide and made up the branch's executive committee; collectively all the elected stewards comprised the branch committee; and the factory's production workers formed the branch membership. In this manner two potentially antagonistic bases of labor representation were meshed together - the official union structure and the system of workplace representation through the shop stewards. (All of these people - apart from the membership - were shop stewards in the sense of the definition given earlier, i.e., they remained employees of the company and received no remuneration from union funds.)

However this apparent structural congruence only masked what was in fact a virtually complete break. The branch did not serve as a transmission belt, either for policy guidelines originating from union congress or headquarters or for rank-and-file views. As Goldthorpe et al. (1968, p.17) found, 'in the eyes of the rank-and-file, the [union] bureaucracy has become irrelevant to the conduct of industrial relations in their particular workplace.'

As far as pay and conditions in the factory were concerned, the union's influence was non-existent. Although the collective agreement covering the factory was nominally concluded between the union and the company it was in fact an entirely internal matter. Annual negotiations were conducted at factory level between management and a committee of shop stewards (the branch executive committee enlarged by the co-optation of two further stewards). No permanent official of the union played any part in the process - in fact in the most recent negotiations the union had not even got a copy of the branch's claim. (9) And while all collective agreements had to be ratified by a secret ballot of the production workers, there was no requirement for them to be approved at any other level. A branch officer said that, while the branch tried to take account of national union policy, it was in practice entirely free to reach whatever settlement it wished.

One vestige of the industry-wide system for the regulation of labor relations that we shall encounter is the provision in the factory's grievance procedure for the involvement of the union's district official at the penultimate stage and for conciliation and arbitration through a joint panel (of union and employers' association representatives) at the final stage. This provision had been invoked several times in the year preceding my visit.

It is fair to say that such influence as the labor representatives enjoyed derived almost entirely from their role as shop stewards and hardly at all from their positions in the branch. Thus, although the turnout in elections for steward/branch officer was about 70 per cent, attendance at branch meetings averaged 1 to 2 per cent. (10) A branch officer observed that there was a general 'lack of interest in the running of the union.' However it should be noted that meetings were held outside work hours (one Sunday morning a month, to be precise). Donovan suggested that interest in branch affairs might be reanimated if meetings were held at the

place of work (which was the case) and, at least when the occasion
demanded, during work hours (op.cit., p.186). As Goldthorpe et al.
found, there was a widespread 'feeling that affairs at branch level
are of little relevance to what goes on in [workers'] particular
shops and factories.... From their point of view the shop steward
was a far more important official than any at branch level' (1968,
pp.102-3).

There was little evidence that the union had attempted to clarify
the constitutional position of the shop steward within its organization. Its rules remained silent on such matters as 'elections,
terms of office, the filling of casual vacancies, the bounds of the
shop steward's jurisdiction, his relations with other union officials and his place in the union's organization' (Donovan, p.272).
(11) These were left to be determined by the shop steward body
itself. In other words the shop steward system in the English factory still bore the imprint of its origins. (12) In Britain this
system has grown up outside the official union structure in response
to pressures, needs and opportunities in the workplace. And it has
remained a 'semi-independent force in the industrial relations
system, with tenuous ties to the old established machinery' (Goodman
and Whittingham, 1969, p.7).

Strikes

At no point is this disjunction between the two systems more evident
than in the question of the authority to initiate a strike. The
vast majority of stoppages in British industry are unofficial (wildcat), i.e., they have not been sanctioned or ratified by the union
or unions whose members are on strike. (13) After a survey of
British union rule books, Weekes et al. (1975, pp.98-100) concluded
that

> Many of them did not define the role and responsibility of all
> officers and officials in industrial action nore, in particular,
> the role of shop stewards.... Most union rule books dealt only
> briefly with the calling or organizing of strikes. The major
> preoccupation ... was the organization, administration and fi-
> nance of the unions.... Most limited the specific strike powers
> to their central bodies, but such a limitation did not generally
> prevent the subsequent support of strikes.... Rules on strikes
> were often only rules about strike funds.

The English factory, as will be seen, was no exception to the rule
that in Britain stoppages take place outside the framework of the
union. Only in the rare case (one will be described later) did
stoppages even come to the official attention of the union.

Shop steward and management in the English factory

If only modest advances had been made since Donovan in formalizing
the role of the shop steward within the union, what was his position
in relation to management? Historically, of course, official contacts were confined to trade unions and employers' associations.
Such bargaining as occurred within the workplace was unofficial or,

at best, semi-official, and rarely had any formal institutions been
developed to conduct it in an orderly, systematic fashion. This
situation had become progressively more untenable as workplace bargaining displaced industry bargaining as the principal determinant
of wages and conditions. Donovan urged an end to 'the pretence of
industry-wide agreements' by putting the relations between management and shop stewards on an official footing.

As we have seen, in addition to asking that union government be
modified to accommodate the shop steward, Donovan proposed that employers acknowledge shop stewards as full negotiating partners and
grant them the necessary facilities to represent the workers. This
could be accomplished through the factory agreement which

can cover the rights and obligations of shop stewards within the
factory. Within the limits of union rules it can set out the
stewards' constituencies and the method of their election. The
facilities for stewards to meet with each other and their chief
steward can be covered, along with the arrangements for meeting
their constituents, access to a telephone and an office, and en-
titlement to pay while performing their jobs as stewards (op.
cit., p.41).

With the important qualification noted above, namely that there
were three separate agreements, Donovan's recommendations regarding
the steward's status in the workplace had been implemented (where
they had not already been in operation). A factory agreement,
negotiated by a committee of shop stewards representing all the
production workers, codified the role of the shop steward in the
factory, spelling out, for example, the number of stewards, their
constituencies, terms of office, and so on. The facilities provided
by the company were generally in line with the most enlightened
practice recommended by the government. (14) These facilities included the following:

-Shop stewards suffered no loss of earnings for any 'reasonable
 time' spent on their activities as representatives. In addition
 the two most senior stewards (the branch chairman and secretary)
 had been relieved of all work responsibilities while continuing
 to receive full pay.

-The company had placed a small office and a conference room permanently at the branch's disposal and other rooms (e.g., cinema,
 sports pavilion) were available when the need arose.

-The company's employment office distributed union membership
 forms to all new hires. ('Our best recruiting officer'.)

-The company operated the check-off (the 'practice whereby employers agree to deduct trade union dues from the wages of members and pay them over to the union concerned,' Donovan, p.192).
 It withheld a five per cent service fee to cover the expense involved so that an arm's length relationship was technically
 maintained.

-Notice-boards were provided for shop stewards to communicate
 with their membership.

-Facilities were provided for branch and shop steward elections.
These elections were conducted during work hours, and ballot
boxes were placed at clocking stations.

It should also be mentioned that the company had acquiesced in the
union's demand for a union shop. In consequence it was a condition
of continued employment that a production worker become a union
member (the so-called post-entry closed shop). Certain workers in
the company's employment before this agreement was reached (those
over 55 or with at least 10 years' service) had been exempted from
its terms and a handful still remained outside the union.

There was provision for regular joint consultation between
management and shop stewards by means of a works council. The
Factory Personnel Manager and the chairman of the union branch were
ex officio respectively chairman and secretary of the works council,
and all elected (15) shop stewards were members of the labor side of
the council. A full council meeting was held at least once quarterly; in addition there were monthly meetings of the council's executive committee. Much of the council's business was actually trans-
acted in a variety of subcommittees. For example, there were monthly meetings of divisional works councils - i.e., meetings of management and stewards in the passenger and truck tire plants respectively - and meetings of various specialist subcommittees concerned with
such matters as safety, pensions, the provision and upkeep of
vending machines, and so on. (16)

The agenda of the full works council might typically include
current production and technical problems, the company's market
situation, sales and production reports, important technical developments, plans to introduce new equipment, etc. In addition, the
works council was consulted when the company wished to institute
short-time working or to carry out lay-offs or dismissals. A branch
officer told me that management 'takes us into its confidence, but
more could be divulged.' The full council also dealt with matters
arising from divisional council meetings which had not been resolved
at that level: at one meeting these matters included ventilation in
the passenger tire plant, pilfering, a report from the Factory
Personnel Manager on the progress of a scheme for facilitating internal transfers, a report from the Good Housekeeping Committee
chairman (a manager) on vandalism, and the branch's recommendations
to management (after a ballot of its membership) concerning the
vacation schedule for the following year. In addition to these
channels for regular consultation there were numerous working parties and ad hoc committees, not to mention contacts in the course of
disciplinary hearings, social occasions and so on.

By and large the activities of the works council appeared to be
appreciated by the production workers and their stewards. Some shop
stewards evidently enjoyed the pastoral duties subcommittee membership often brought; another said the meetings were better than
working. However there was an unmistakable sense that such activities were at best a secondary part of the steward's role. As the
tire room steward explained, 'the works council has no teeth; you
can only recommend.' The raison d'être of the shop steward was bargaining for his members back in his department. (17) In other
words, in spite of an array of formal institutions designed to
enable the stewards to participate in the government of the work-

place, the traditional conception of them as 'essentially shop-floor bargainers' (McCarthy, 1966, p.30) still had a very tenacious hold.

Conclusion

It is clear that in many important respects Donovan's recommendations had been implemented in the English factory, or alternatively they had already long been in force. In any case they appeared to have had little impact on the role of the shop steward. As we shall see, the gears of the formal machinery of workplace representation had failed to engage the issued of burning concern on the shop floor, whatever the system's merits on paper.

WORKPLACE LABOR ORGANIZATION IN GERMANY

What Ross called the 'shift in the center of gravity' in Western European labor relations was also evident in Germany. The crucial difference is that the shift to the level of the plant found the German system prepared. Even before this process had been set in motion by full employment there existed in the German workplace established, and highly formalized, machinery for the representation of labor, namely the works council. Insofar as it occurred, then, the shift involved a transfer of power from one system of labor representation - the trade unions - to another - the works council.

The works council

Without providing a comprehensive account of the place of the works council in the German system of labor relations, (18) it is necessary to point out certain distinctive features of this institution that have a direct bearing on the present discussion. First, the works council (Betriebsrat) is not a union body. It is elected by all the employees in a workplace irrespective of union membership. The relations of the works council to the union will be examined later in this chapter. Second, the form of the works council and its rights and obligations are comprehensively defined by statute. (19) Let us take this last point first.

Form and functions of the works council

In Britain, as Flanders (1968, p.78) has observed, it is customary to deal with industrial disputes 'by trying to find an acceptable compromise rather than by a "lawyer's decision" depending on the interpretation of words.' In Germany, by contrast, labor relations are regulated by an apparently seamless web of laws (and quasi-laws, since collective agreements have the force of law). This fact has often been remarked upon, not always favorably. (20) According to Spiro (1958:10), it reflects 'an attitude which may be described as faith in the feasibility of "institutional engineering."' In the following sections we shall see that that faith may not have been

misplaced. More striking than the existence of these laws is the
extent to which they do actually regulate day-to-day relations in
German industry. (21)

In the workplace the law fixes the size, composition, duties and
powers of the works council. In the factory that I visited, the
council comprised eleven employees (two of whom were white-collar).
Under the law all the employees in the factory, barring a few senior
managers (leitende Angestellte), were entitled to vote in the works
council elections. However, blue- and white-collar works councillors were elected in separate ballots. (22) Voting is by secret
ballot for candidates nominated by the employees; (23) the life of
the works council is three years. The members of the newly elected
council in turn elect a chairman and deputy chairman. The law requires that a number of councillors (how many depends on the size of
the establishment; there were two in this case) be relieved of
their work responsibilities so that they may attend full-time to
their duties as representatives. In addition other councillors are
entitled to such time off with full pay as is required by their
duties. (24) To prevent victimization, councillors enjoy special
protection against dismissal which extends beyond their terms of
office. Unlike the shop steward who might be recalled from his
office on the petition of 75 per cent of his constituents, the works
councillor has virtually complete security of tenure. Removal from
office, or dissolution of the council, requires a finding by a labor
court that the councillor(s) have been guilty of 'gross dereliction
of their legal duties.' All expenses of the council (e.g., office
space, supplies, telephone, etc.) are borne by the employer.

The chairman of the works council may convene meetings as often
as he likes provided that 25 per cent of the councillors desire such
a meeting. At least once monthly the council must meet with management. And at least once quarterly the chairman must convene a factory assembly; and he must invite the employer who may also address
the assembly. The employer must present a report on certain matters
(set out in the act) to the assembly at least once yearly.

Most of the day-to-day business of the council is conducted in
committees meeting with managerial counterparts. The most important
of these committees is the executive committee which is empowered to
act for the council in all matters short of formal plant agreements.
Again its size and responsibilities are fixed by law. Among the
other committees, the piecework, economic, and social committees
deserve mention.

The 'general duties of the works council' include supervising the
observance by the employer of the terms of laws, regulations, collective agreements, etc. in the interests of the employees, propos-
ing to the employer measures for the benefit of the enterprise and
the workforce, and caring particularly for the interests of those in
need of special protection (the young, old, handicapped, and
foreigners). The council is obligated to take up with management
the grievances of employees provided it considers them justified.

The works council is granted a number of statutory rights in the
workplace to enable it to discharge these duties. These rights are
of different weights depending on the issue involved. In respect of
some matters the council merely has a right to be informed; in
others it has to be consulted; and in still others it has the right

of co-determination. These classes of rights broadly correspond to
three categories of issues: economic, personnel, and social.

For example, the council enjoys the right of co-determination
over certain social matters: disciplinary rules, the scheduling of
the work-day and work-breaks, the introduction and use of equipment
for monitoring workers' behavior or performance, overtime or temporary short-working, workplace social amenities, holiday arrangements, questions of wage and salary administration, especially the
establishment of the principles of remuneration and the introduction
and application of new and changed systems of payment, etc. Of particular interest for the present discussion, the council has the
right of co-determination over the setting of piecerates.

In addition the council has rights regarding matters of personnel
policy. Thus the employer is required to inform the council about
current and future manpower needs and to consult with it on ways to
avoid consequent hardships. The employer's policies with respect to
recruitment, dismissal, transfers and reclassifications require approval by the council. In individual cases the council may withhold
its consent under conditions spelt out in the Works Constitution
Act.

An economic committee (nominated by the council but not necessarily restricted to councillors) is entitled to be informed on a
range of economic questions. These include the economic and financial situation of the company, production and sales figures, production and investment programs, changes in production techniques and
work methods, etc. and any other plans that could materially affect
the interest of employees.

The employer is also required to consult with the council on any
major changes that could entail hardships for the workforce. Such
changes include a substantial rundown or suspension of operations,
a transfer of operations, plant closure, merger, fundamental changes
in work methods, and so on. In such cases the council and the employer may have to agree on a social plan to alleviate the hardships. Thus when half the factory's workforce was dismissed following the oil crisis in 1974, a social plan had been drawn up
which, among other things, fixed the scale of severance payments
and determined the order in which employees were dismissed in the
light of social considerations such as their ages and family situations.

In the event of disputes between council and employer over
matters subject to co-determination, the law provides for their resolution by mediation and arbitration. In the normal case this involves an ad hoc conciliation committee of equal numbers of council
and management representatives together with an impartial chairman
who may, if necessary, be appointed by the labor court. (25) In
certain circumstances (e.g., disputes over dismissals) there is provision for compulsory arbitration by the labor court, and in other
cases (e.g., disputes over the appropriate labor grade for a particular job) a question may be referred to the union and employers'
association for settlement.

Before we leave this subject, two further aspects of labor representation should be mentioned. The first is the presence of a
worker representative on the company's supervisory board (Aufsichts-
rat), where he was one of three directors. In this case the worker

director happened to be the same person as the works council chairman.   The second is the company-wide or general works council
(Gesamtbetriebsrat) responsible for issues concerning the company
as a whole or several of its establishments.   Since most of the company's employees worked in the factory, this body was largely an extension of the factory works council.   Neither of these institutions
will be examined in detail because they impinge only marginally on
the workplace itself.

The union in the workplace

As Ross points out, 'inside the establishment ... the crucial fact
is that the German labor union does not have a formal existence'
(1962, p.344).   Under the law the functions of workplace representation have been pre-empted by the works council.   In the resulting
two-tier system the union's main role is as a bargaining agent in
negotiations with the employers' association;   in fact the union is
not recognized by the individual employer;   its relations are confined to its counterpart, the employers' association.   In the words
of two critics of the system, the Works Constitution Act of 1952
'consolidated the power of the entrepreneur and evicted the trade
unions from the plant' (Bergmann and Mueller-Jentsch, 1975, p.242).
The structure of the German union reflects this fact: the lowest
level of union organization is not the workplace but the local
branch (Ortsverwaltung) consisting of members of the union according
to their place of residence (in this way it resembles the usual
British situation).   Union officials have right of access to a workplace provided they give notice of their visit to the employer.
However this access is granted only for purposes expressly sanctioned by law.   They may attend works council meetings if their
presence is requested by one quarter of its members;   but such invi-
tations appear to be rare (Sturmthal, 1964, p.69).
   This expulsion of the union from the workplace might have been
less of a cause for concern had it not been for the shift in the
center of gravity alluded to earlier.   In theory the monopoly on
collective bargaining might have given the German unions substantial
influence over pay and conditions in the workplace;   particularly in
view of the comprehensive scope of German collective agreements.
(26)   Just as the law limits the unions' role in the workplace so it
expressly reserves to the unions the right to negotiate on matters
'customarily regulated by collective agreement.'   However, the post-
war years have seen a growing tendency for actual earnings and conditions to be determined in the workplace.   As Reichel (1973, p.110)
has noted:
   At the insistence of the unions the law provides that decisions
   on wages and other conditions of employment which already have
   been, or customarily are, settled by collective agreement may not
   be included in the plant agreement.   Nevertheless it frequently
   does happen that work councils obtain concessions from management, including concessions on wages which do not properly fall
   within the sphere allotted to them by law.
As a consequence, 'the terms set in [collective] agreements are
usually not the actual terms of employment, particularly not in the

area of wages. They are minima.... Actual rates ... are normally
above the contract rates. The contract sets a floor upon which the
effective wage structure is erected.... The distance ... is often
considerable. Unions ... are greatly concerned about the fact since
it, in effect, transfers the task of effective wage bargaining
wholly or partly to the works councils' (Sturmthal, 1964, pp.76-7).
(27)

The unions' alarm is traceable to a number of different causes.
First, the payments in excess of the contractual rates do not enjoy
the same legal protection as do the contractual rates themselves.
'Concessions made to the councils are revocable; those embodied in
collective agreements with the unions are legally binding' (Sturmthal, 1964, p.164). As we shall see, the works council is statu-
torily debarred from striking and so is in a weak position to protect these gains. A second consideration is that the growing gap
between actual and negotiated rates might weaken workers' interest
in collective bargaining and in trade unionism in general. There
has, in fact, been a consistent decline in the density of union
membership over the years (though this trend may have been arrested
in 1970). (28) The resulting enterprise chauvinism (Betriebs-
egoismus) might endanger the solidarity of the labor movement and
so put at risk past and future gains. 'In the case of a strike, the
distance between the effective wage rate and that which the union
aims at may be such that the relevance of the union demand for the
improvement of the worker's standard is far from being clear to him'
(Sturmthal, 1964, p.161). Finally, there is unquestionably concern
on the part of union officialdom at its loss of influence following
the shift of the center of gravity to the workplace. (29)

In these circumstances, it is not surprising that 'the more aggressive unions are attempting to push themselves within the plant
gates and break through the judicial wall which formally separates
them from the works councils' (Ross, 1962, pp.345-6). Actually the
unions are not without resources to make their influence felt in the
workplace. First, the union normally draws up a slate of candidates
for election to the council and 'apparently these slates are almost
always elected' (Ross, 1962, p.346). (30) The overwhelming majority
of councillors are union designees: 80 per cent of those elected in
1975 were union members. Second, the councils rely heavily on the
unions for expert advice and training. Third, the union commonly
has its own unofficial representatives in the workplace (Vertrauensleute - literally men of trust) who may exert pressure on the council to remain faithful to union policies (see Bergmann et al., 1975,
p.303).

Nevertheless the councils have generally retained a substantial
degree of autonomy. Doubtless this is attributable to a number of
circumstances, among which are the council's legal independence, the
obligations imposed on it by the law, its answerability to its constituency in the workplace, and the scope for autonomous policies in
the workplace created by full employment. Consequently there has
been barely concealed frustration in union circles, and at various
times strategies have been proposed to strengthen the unions' influence in the workplace. (31) One approach that holds particular
interest is the attempt to bypass the works council by strengthening
the position of the Vertrauensleute. Barkin (1975, p.386) states

flatly that 'the ultimate union goal is to replace the works councils with union agencies.' But, at least as a tactical measure, the
unions have limited their demands to obtaining for the Vertrauensleute the same protections as are enjoyed by council members. Their
hopes that the new Works Constitution Act would take the first steps
in this direction were disappointed, (32) and they have not made
headway towards this objective through collective bargaining. Moreover the attempt to create beachheads in the workplace has, on occasion, led to strained relations with the works councils. 'In
practice, the relationship between council and [Vertrauensleute] is
not always harmonious. Works councils are known to have felt ...
that the [Vertrauensmann] as representative of the union is an outsider who interferes with the settlement of industrial relations
problems "within the family"' (Sturmthal, 1964, p.73).

Strikes

In Germany the right to strike is closely circumscribed by law. For
one thing, the works council may not call a strike (though its members may participate in a strike duly called by the union). The
Works Constitution Act enjoins both council and employer to abstain
from 'measures of labor struggle' and other actions that interfere
with normal working or disturb the peace in the workplace. It follows that wildcat strikes are ipso facto illegal, and workers who
take part in them are liable to instant dismissal and claims for
damages.
    The right to call a strike (or a lockout) is a prerogative of
parties capable of entering into a collective agreement (this generally means unions and employers' associations). Even then, to meet
the test of legality, strikes must satisfy certain stringent conditions: (i) A strike is illegal if it is conducted during the cur-
rency of a collective agreement. (ii) It is illegal if it is called
before all peaceful remedies have been exhausted (i.e., it must be a
last resort or ultima ratio). (iii) It is illegal if it is not directed at some object susceptible of regulation by collective agreement; thus political and sympathy strikes are outlawed. (iv) Under
the doctrine of proportionality (Verhältnismässigkeit), a strike is
illegal if it is aimed at inflicting lasting damage on the adversary. (33)
    Certain additional factors may limit strikes in Germany. The
unions themselves generally have strict rules respecting the initia-
tion and continuation of strikes. 'As a matter of principle, a
majority of 75 per cent must support the strike at any stage. The
ultimate power to call the strike lies with the national board and
is not a matter for the regional board representing the bargaining
unit concerned' (Schmidt, 1972, p.46). As a matter of fact, the
chemical workers' union (IG Chemie), apparently alone among major
German unions, has amended its constitution to permit its leadership
to call a strike without first holding a secret ballot. Another
factor that may discourage strikes is their cost: 'With bargaining
on an industry-wide basis, a strike tends to throw out of work a
large proportion of the union membership at one time. The expense
of such a widespread strike is made very great because of the prac-

tice of union payment of high strike benefits' (Kerr, 1957, p.188).
In addition, and in contrast to the British practice, the government
pays no social security benefits to strikers' families so as not to
become party to the dispute.

The works council in practice

The works council in the factory investigated in this study did not
depart in any significant respect from the situation depicted in the
preceding paragraphs. However certain details may be usefully added
to round out the picture.
    The composition of the works council sheds light on its role in
the workplace. Its members were appreciably older than the rest of
the workforce (five of the eleven were over 50) and tended to have
the longest service records with the company. Only two of the councillors were production workers, only one a guest worker (a Turk),
and one was a woman. (34)
    What does the make-up of the council reveal? The first thing to
be noted is what Sturmthal calls 'the predominance of the "father"
type.'
    Paternalistic traits are inherent in the outlook of the people
    involved as well as in the actual operation of the system. The
    councillors treat the workers in a paternalistic way and are
    usually expected to do so.... The significant fact is that in
    many cases the works council has ... become a partner in a
    management team which administers the labor force of the enter-
    prise with authority and benevolence (1964, p.68).
    The overrepresentation on the council of skilled workers (i.e.,
engineers as opposed to production workers) may have reflected a
cultural deference towards expertise. On the other hand, it is
likely that this relationship would be washed out if age and nationality were controlled for. (Germans made up over 90 per cent of the
engineers, but only 50 per cent of the production workers; engineers tended to be older and to have longer service.)
    Such a deference may also have been at work in the choice of the
council chairman. It will be recalled that the council elects one
of its members as chairman. In this case it had chosen one of the
two white-collar councillors. The man in question was young (late
30s) and something of an intellectual. However it is possible that
this cultural trait, viz. the deference to expertise, had a sound
pragmatic basis. After all, the point has already been made that
day-to-day labor relations in Germany are pervasively conditioned
by the law. In such circumstances it is not surprising that a pre-
mium may be placed on analytical and dialectical abilities. In fact
many discussions between management and council turned on the interpretation of some clause in the collective agreement or in a statute. The shelves of the offices of the works council and of the
Personnel Manager were well stocked with copies of the relevant
statutes. (35)
    The preponderance of older councillors probably also reflected
the fact that 'it is not always easy to find good candidates in sufficient number among the younger men' (Sturmthal, 1964, p.68). The
election was not hotly contested and attracted a turn-out of only 50

per cent of the work force. (36)   Membership of the council appeared
to be looked upon as a responsibility to be taken on by the civic-
minded employees.

Council and management had good working relations.   At least over
the four previous years, they had been able to resolve all their
differences without recourse to outside mediation or arbitration.
What was striking about these relations, at least in contrast with
the English factory, was their formality.   The banter often exchanged by shop stewards and managers in the English factory was
largely absent.   Moreover this difference reached too deep in the
factory to be explained away as the outcome of personality. (37)

Apart from flyers on high-minded topics like aid to the third
world, the union had no visible presence in the factory.   However,
all but one of the works councillors were union members, and the
chairman appeared to be the most active unionist in the factory.
There was no separate corps of Vertrauensleute and therefore no
opportunity for the sort of friction alluded to earlier.

CONCLUSION

In this chapter we have seen how, in both Britain and Germany, post-
war conditions undermined the regulatory power of industry agreements by vastly increasing the scope and opportunities for bargaining at the factory level.   These same centrifugal forces, however,
did not simply shift bargaining power from industry to factory, but
also led to its dispersal within the factory.   It is the consequences of the altered power relations inside the workplace that
form the interest of this study.

These consequences have not been the same in the two countries.
In Britain they have contributed to the breakdown of government in
the workplace, both of management and of labor representatives.
This, in turn, it will be argued, has unleashed intense sectional
rivalries on the shop floor.   In the absence of effective structures
for integrating the interests of different groups of workers, these
rivalries have spiralled out of control in a war of all against all.

In Germany, on the other hand, the system of labor relations has
been able to withstand the new strains.   The disruptive effects of
the dispersal of bargaining power have been held in check.   This has
been made possible, it will be argued, by the existence of means for
the resolution of differences - and potential differences - without
resort to a trial of strength.

Chapter 4

DISORDER IN THE WORKPLACE

The argument of this study, it will be recalled, is that a breakdown of government in the British workplace has led to widespread industrial disorder, and that this disorder, in turn, accounts for Britain's economic weakness. In this chapter two questions are taken up. First, what forms does the disorder in British industry take? Second, how does this disorder affect productivity? The remaining question, the sources of the breakdown of industrial order, is deferred to later chapters. This chapter, then, is primarily concerned with the state of labor relations in the English factory; comparative materials from the German factory are introduced only to highlight certain contrasts.

FRACTIONAL BARGAINING

Neither the English nor the German factory had experienced a full-blown strike in living memory. Thus when I speak of disorder in the English factory I am referring to something quite different from set-piece battles between massed armies of employers and workers; instead I mean the presence there of endemic fractional bargaining. This term is borrowed from James W. Kuhn (1961). Fractional bargaining is distinguished from collective bargaining, in the normal usage of that term, by the fact that it is conducted by a group of workers rather than by an official bargaining unit. It is aimed at securing the ends of the work group rather than of, say, the local; and it is conducted in disregard of, and perhaps in breach of, the procedures agreed by the official labor representatives and the employer. Fractional bargaining is engaged in by union members; however it involves them 'only as members of work groups, not as union members. The union representatives participate more as the leaders of their work groups than as union leaders' (ibid., p.79).
    When does a number of workers constitute a work group? According to Kuhn, the work group is defined by technology. The worker 'need not seek out other workers who share his daily work interests since the technology of his work usually places him in a group whose job interests follow a common pattern' (ibid., p.131). 'The members of the group jointly perform or share a certain task in the production

process. It is a regular and stable unit (1) within factory society, delimited by a given technology' (ibid.).

In Kuhn's view, if there is one crucial reason why fractional
bargaining may arise in a workplace it is that the balance of power
has shifted in favor of the work group (or of certain strategically
placed work groups). Fractional bargaining exists 'because [work
groups] have the ability to raise the cost of disagreeing and lower
the cost of agreeing to their terms' (ibid., p.79). The same
rational calculus explains why workers participate in fractional
bargaining: it 'must promise enough benefits from management at low
enough cost to the group members to keep unenthusiastic members from
actively resisting the action' (ibid., p.109). The shift of power
also largely suffices to explain the transformation of the work
group 'an sich' into the work group 'für sich:' 'The willingness of
workers to engage in fractional bargaining arises ... also from the
power-based expectations of the workers' (ibid., p.144).

In the modern factory, power commonly resides with the work
group, as opposed to the individual worker or the local union:' (2)

Refractory problems present themselves in managing a plant and
running a unified local union ... if the members of a work group
support shop bargaining and the use of disruptive tactics. Tactics involving a work group as a whole greatly enlarge the range
of coercion. If a single worker or even a very few workers stop
working, slow down, refuse overtime work, or snarl up special
jobs, management may at worst be inconvenienced but not coerced
into an undesired concession. If all the workers of a whole department use any of those tactics, management may well be forced
to submit unwillingly....

Some work groups can secure gains through fractional bargaining that even the local union cannot obtain. They can do so because the bargaining power available to them is not dependent
upon the bargaining power of the local union in plant negotiations (or even of the international union in firm-wide negotiations). The bargaining power of the various work groups ... is
not a simple fraction of the total bargaining power of the local
union.... Some groups have more strength to enforce *their* demands than the whole union has to enforce *its* demands, and some
have less. The weaker groups must depend on the local union to
get such benefits as they enjoy. Not so the stronger groups;
these can act quite independently of the local, deciding
autonomously upon their fractional bargaining tactics and
seeking their own goals (ibid., p.99).

The power of the work group derives primarily from certain technological conditions. 'The ability of the work group to conduct
fractional bargaining depends upon the power relationship between
the work group, the union, and management, a relationship significantly influenced by the technological conditions under which a
plant or industry operates' (ibid., p.145). Among these conditions
the most important is the existence of 'continuous, rigidly sequen-
tial processing of materials into one major type of product.' Such
a technology 'enables the work group to disrupt the plant's total
production at a cost to itself which is small in relation to the
cost it inflicts upon management.' 'The more vulnerable the total
production is to disruption ... the greater the power of groups to

demand their terms of settlement whatever the provisions of the
agreement or the understandings of top union and management officials' (ibid., p.148).

It is in the nature of fractional bargaining, according to Kuhn,
that 'work groups strive ... for settlements that benefit themselves
even if they may injure other work groups. Each may seek to enlarge
the area of work in its own job classification, to raise its members' earnings or lessen its members' work effort, to restrict
bumping in from other groups, and to gain any special job privilege
it can' (ibid., p.134). As a consequence, 'other groups may either
take it upon themselves to recoup their losses through their own
fractional bargaining or to retaliate against the first group'
(ibid., p.109).

Finally it is worth recording that fractional bargaining usually
takes place in face of the opposition of the official union leadership: 'Almost without exception leaders in all of the local unions
... denounced work stoppages and genuinely co-operated with the
international unions and with management to discourage them' (ibid.,
p.104). However, their influence was limited: 'When members of a
work group become dissatisfied, they can produce their own *shop*
leader, they do not have to borrow one from the union hall. The
president of a local union may counsel his members and mediate
grievance disputes, but he does not necessarily have the authority
to forbid the use of this or that tactic of fractional bargaining'
(ibid., p.105).

It will be noted that Kuhn has identified another factor - technology - tending to inflate the power of the work group. To recapitulate then: a variety of circumstances, some originating in
the post-war years (labor shortages, full order books), and others
which are prolongation of trends long underway (the growing interdependence of operations within the plant, capital-intensive technology), (3) have contributed to the dispersal of power in the
workplace, i.e., they have created conditions highly favorable to
the growth of fractional bargaining.

These trends have been no less marked in Germany than in
Britain: labor shortages have been acuter; demand has been at
least as strong; and German industry is more highly capitalized.
Consequently German industry should be no less susceptible - perhaps marginally more so - to fractional bargaining. There is in
fact some indirect evidence that fractional bargaining may be on
the increase in Germany: the share of all strikes accounted for by
wildcats has doubled in the period 1949-53 to 1964-68 (Bergmann et
al., 1975, p.322). However neither in relative nor in absolute
terms has the German level approached the British. And, indeed, in
the German factory selected for study fractional bargaining proved
to be practically non-existent, while in the English factory it had
reached epidemic proportions.

Fractional bargaining tactics in the British factory

The most conspicuous form of fractional bargaining pressure adopted
by groups of workers in the English factory was, of course, the work
stoppage. An analysis of the stoppages in the passenger tire plant

over a two-year period is presented in Table 4.1. It will be
noticed that the typical stoppage involved a small number of workers
- a single department or a fraction of a department. It was of
short duration - over 75 per cent did not outlive the shift in which
they had started. It is also of interest that not a single department was stoppage-free in either of the two years. All these
actions were unconstitutional (in that they were taken before the
agreed grievance procedures had run their course) and unofficial
(in the sense that they had not been authorized by the production
workers' union at branch or any other level). (4) An account of the
most serious of the stoppages in the tire room in the course of 1977
- the 'X' machine case - is given in the next section.

However, wildcat strikes - i.e., actual suspensions of work -
were but the most visible manifestation of the fractional bargaining
in the English factory. They were supplemented by a wide variety of
other pressures - what Flanders has called 'cut-price industrial
action.' (5) For example, at the time of my field work various
forms of pressure were being applied by different groups in the tire
room: the tirebuilders were operating a ban on overtime and weekend
working that was already eight years old; the tire room servicemen
were refusing to return defective materials to the stock preparation
departments, charging that this was not part of their negotiated job
description; for three weeks the factory's supervisors 'withdrew
their co-operation' - among other things, this meant that they refused to cover for absent colleagues (of whom there were more than
usual) and also refused to report machine breakdowns by telephone;
(6) these actions, it may be noted, came on top of a policy of two
years' standing of not accepting any responsibilities that were not
part of their traditional duties; on the eve of my departure it
appeared that Technical Division personnel were withholding machines
from production (ostensibly on technical grounds) in furtherance of
a claim of their own; a number of machines were being operated
below capacity (and had been for months) because of the inability
of management and the builders involved to agree on the appropriate
piecerates. In other departments, so far as it was possible to
ascertain, the picture was largely the same.

These practices may at one time have been isolated pressure tactics, but by the time of my visit they were settling into routines
on the shop floor. In fact it was increasingly difficult to tell
where fractional bargaining ended and normal working began. The
consequences this had for the operation of the factory will be
looked at later in this chapter. However, the losses from fractional bargaining prompted the managing director to make the following remarks to the factory newspaper a year after my fieldwork
was completed:

Unofficial disputes are making our financial position critical.
The fact is [that the company's] employees are among the best-
paid in the district and in the industry, but we still do not
have settled industrial relations and steady production.

Work disruptions, caused by a failure to keep disputes inside
the procedure agreed between the Company and the Union helps
[sic] only our competitors, including those from overseas.

Unless the factory produces the tyres our customers need, we
will be unable to meet our expenses or find money to re-invest

TABLE 4.1   English passenger tire plant. Work stoppages - 1976 and 1977

No.	Date	No. of workers involved	Length of stoppage	Department struck	Reason reported
1	1976 13 Jan.	7	1 hour	C	Disputed piecework rate.
2	30 Jan.	28	3-4 hours	G&H	'Inadequate heating.'
3	1 Feb.	41	2½-3 hours	D	Scheduled work complete. Operators refuse to clean equipment for balance of shift because pay would be less than piecework.
4	2 Feb.	18	2½ hours	B	Dispute over piecework rate on experimental job.
5	19 Feb.	12	1¼ hours	D	Protest against audit of recording of times and pieces by industrial engineers.
6	8 Mar.	24	4 hours	D	Claim for special rate for experimental work.
7	17-19 Mar.	1113	3 days	Whole plant	Stoppage in support of claim for compensation for earnings lost because of disruptions caused by engineers' work-to-rule.
8	? Jun.	484	1-5 hours	6 depts	'Operators refused to work due to current heat wave.'
9	5 Jul.	20	½ hour	A	Crew refuses to work because asked to meet stringent quality standards with malfunctioning equipment.
10	2 Aug.	6	1 hour	C	Servicemen protest at loss of earnings caused by stoppages by other workers.
11	6 Aug.	240	20 hours	E (tire room)	Tirebuilders claim for earnings lost when they had to service own machines. Servicemen had not prepared start-up on Sunday night.

No.	Date	Number	Duration	Dept	Description
12	31 Aug.	10	1 hour	F	'Dissatisfaction at rates.'
13	8 Sep.	12	3½ hours	D	Claim for earnings lost due to 'excessive downtime' (presumably mechanical or scheduling failures).
14	23 Sep.	81	c.2 hours	G&H	Claim for earnings lost due to power failure.
15	24 Sep.	34	½ hour	D	Pay dispute affecting one crew. Whole dept stops work.
16	27 Sep.	244	8 hours	E (tire room)	Dispute over rate payable when materials are substandard.
17	5-9 Oct.	–	4 days	All depts	Consequential lay-off following strike by staff and supervisory personnel.
18	5 Nov.	77	¼ hour	E (tire room)	Discussion of rate proposed by management.
19	24 Nov.	30	20 hours	F	Dispute over modification to equipment.
20	3 Dec.	116	4½ hours	D	Dispute over piecework rate.
21	1977 3 Jan.	62	5½ hours	E (tire room)	Claim for earnings lost because of delays following post-vacation factory start-up.
22	4 Jan.	14	1½ hours	A	Claim for earnings lost due to preceding stoppage.
23	27 Jan.	19	1 hour	B	Claim for earnings lost due to equipment delays.
24	3 Feb.	68	½ hour	E (tire room)	Dispute over rate (two ¼-hour meetings).
25	? Feb.	80	1 hour	E (tire room)	Dispute over condition of material.
26	? Feb.	37	1½ hours	D	Claim for earnings lost while engineers carried out alterations to equipment.
27	9-21 Mar.	340	8 days	E (tire room)	Dispute over rate for 'X' machine and over management insistence rate be worked for trial period (see discussion of this dispute).

TABLE 4.1 (continued)

No.	Date	No. of workers involved	Length of stoppage	Department struck	Reason reported
28	1977 21 Mar.	18	2 hours	B	Dispute over appropriate allowance for extra work required by sub-standard materials.
29	22 Mar.	108	24 hours	B	Token stoppage over preceding dispute. Also demand for payment for 21 March 1977 stoppage.
30	26 Mar.	12	2 hours	D	Refusal to be re-assigned when own work halted by absence of internal transport.
31	28 Mar.	12	1 hour	D	Demand for payment for preceding stoppage.
32	23 May	72	1 hour	E (tire room)	Dispute over fall-back rate.
33	24 May	24	1 hour	E (tire room)	Claim by servicemen for earnings lost because of restrictions placed on output by builders.
34	25 May	82	$1\frac{1}{4}$ hours	E (tire room)	Dispute over fall-back rate.
35	27 May	22	6 hours	E (tire room)	Servicemen claim for earnings lost because of boiler breakdown.
36	27 May	81	5 hours	E (tire room)	Tirebuilders refuse to service own machines (?).
37	29 Jun.	80	2 hours	E (tire room)	Meeting over 'X' machine rate.
38	4 Jul.	90	5-6 hours	F	'Excessive heat.'
39	16 Aug.	17	$5\frac{1}{2}$ hours	B	Dispute over payment for delays following factory start-up after vacation.

No.	Date	Number	Duration	Department	Cause
40	1 Sep.	114	21½ hours	B	Dispute over application of guarantee payment during staff and supervisory work-to-rule.
41	18 Oct.	232	22 hours	E (tire room)	Stoppage over management refusal to pay operator for failure to work a new rate for trial period.
42	20-26 Oct.	369	4 days	F, G&H	Claim for compensation for earnings lost due to dispute No. 41.
43	27 Oct.	30	½ hour	C	Protest over lost earnings due to stoppage No. 42.
44	8-15 Nov.*	–	3 days (average)	Another part of factory	Lay-offs caused by a stoppage in Banbury dept (not in passenger plant) resulting in shortage of milled rubber compound.
45	23 Nov.	13	1½ hours	C	Protest against reduction of 'ticket' on certain jobs.
	December 1977		No returns available		

* Exact duration varied from department to department.

Note: Nos 17 and 44 were not stoppages by production workers in the passenger tire plant, but were lay-offs resulting from the actions of other workers.

in the future. Without investment in new equipment, it will be
impossible for us to stay in business on a competitive basis....
     If only I could make every man and woman in the plant realize
that these problems are our OPPORTUNITIES. We can produce the
finest tyres in the world here in Britain and yet we still cannot
get them out of the factory in the numbers needed or at the right
cost or at the right time.

An appendix to this chapter takes up the question of how representative the experience of the English factory is of British industry in
general.

The 'X' Machine case

As may be seen from Table 4.1, the most serious stoppage in the tire
room in 1977 arose out of a dispute over a proposed piecework rate.
(7) It is worth examining this dispute in detail for the light it
sheds on fractional bargaining in the English factory. Since it
occurred before my fieldwork I have drawn on management files to
reconstruct the background, the sequence of events leading up to
the stoppage, and finally the protracted denouement of the dispute.
The files were supplemented by the recollections of some of the key
participants.

Background to the dispute
In the course of 1976 five new tirebuilding machines had been introduced into the tire room. Although they were in fact only modifications of certain existing machines, these machines involved a
radical change in the way in which a tire was built. Without going
into details, it is sufficient to note that the new machines were
widely perceived by management and builders alike as the wave of the
future.

     Management had taken considerable pains to prepare the ground for
the introduction of the new machines. In addition to the customary
processes of consultation, the company had arranged for three production workers - the branch chairman and secretary and one of the
prospective builders - to accompany the production director on a
visit to another of the company's European factories where the 'X'
machine was already operational. (The factory in question was not
the German factory, although the itinerary was extended to take it
in as well; it had been the production director's previous
posting.)

     In the face of shopfloor insistence that the 'X' machines be
manned strictly according to seniority, management had backed down
from its original claim for discretion in making the assignments and
had given the five most senior builders on each shift first refusal
on the new machines.

Setting piecework rates for the 'X' machines
The decisions regarding which builders were to man the 'X' machines
had been made in December 1976. One month earlier management had
issued an 'Industrial Relations News Bulletin' reminding the department of the agreed procedures for establishing piecework rates. It
is unlikely that the timing was accidental. The bulletin is reproduced virtually in its entirety:

NEW AND REVISED PIECEWORK RATES

Considerable time and thought has been given in the past to the
best means by which new and revised piecework rates can be implemented.

The procedure detailed in the Company/Union Agreement ... has
been summarized and illustrated below.

The said procedure will continue to be applied by both parties. It is essential that all parties concerned are familiar
with [the] Agreement.

1 A rate proposal is prepared by Industrial Engineers and presented to the Department Manager concerned.
2 The proposal is ... given to the [shop steward] for him to
   inform the operators concerned. One week is normally allowed
   for this....
4 If the rate is accepted it is noted by the [steward] and
   becomes permanent, with the proviso that queries can be
   raised in the first four weeks of implementation.
5 If the proposal is rejected, the divisional manager and the
   union convenor are notified....
6 If the rate is disputed and further discussion [is] necessary,
   operators will, using the rate, work on a piecework basis for
   a fair period of trial of twenty working days.... Discussions
   will take place on the findings of the trial. If agreement is
   reached the rate becomes permanent. Any ... increases will be
   made retroactive....
7 If agreement [still] cannot be reached, the matter [will] be
   referred to the Factory Personnel Manager. Failure to agree
   at this level [will result in the dispute being] referred to
   an independent panel of the National Joint Industrial Council.
N.B. Should any queries arise in relation to the procedural
agreement, kindly refer those queries to production management or
union representatives [i.e., shop stewards].

Factory Personnel Manager
4 November 1976

In point of fact, the actual provisions of the company/union agreement concerning piecework rates (of which this bulletin purported to
be a summary) were less ambiguous on the question of who was entitled to reject a proposed rate at stage 2. In the original text
the rate is given to the shop steward 'for him to propose to the
operators involved,' not as above, 'for him to inform the operators
concerned.' However, in all other respects the summary was faithful
to the original.

As soon as builders had been assigned to the 'X' machines, the
industrial engineers began intensive time studies. The rate proposed by management (so far only a single high volume tire size was
involved) on completion of the studies was quickly rejected after
consultation between the shop steward and the 'X' builders. The
intervention of the convenor/branch chairman and the divisional
manager (at stage 5) brought no change in the situation. Consequently management determined to invoke their right (stage 6 of
the agreement) to require that the proposed rate be worked for a
20-day trial period.

It is worth pausing here to mention a circumstance that appears

to have contributed to the builders' militancy over the proposed
rate. Some while before these events, another machine, incorporating the same principle as the 'X' machine, had been introduced
into the tire room on an experimental basis but had been discon-
tinued shortly thereafter. Management had agreed to a rate for
this machine which, in the view of the industrial engineers I
talked to, had been extremely loose; in accepting the rate, I was
told, management had 'created a rod for its own back.' The sus-
picion (mistaken, so far as I could tell) was voiced by some of the
builders that the machine had been withdrawn on account of the rate.
In any case, this rate had become a sort of target for the 'X'
builders, and the proposal by management was deemed to fall far
short of it.

Wildcat strike
A deadlock followed as the builders would not budge from their
demand for a more generous rate and baulked at working the trial
period as well. By the beginning of March, after further fruitless
negotiations, management decided to go ahead and apply the trial
period unilaterally. Thereupon the tire room as a whole went out
on strike. Within one day the rest of the passenger tire plant had
been idled by the stoppage.

    The strike lasted from 9 to 21 March. The return to work was ob-
tained largely through the efforts of the convenor/branch chairman.
The basis on which work was resumed was as follows: management
agreed to waive its demand for the 20-day trial period, and the dispute was referred without further delay to a panel of the National
Joint Industrial Council for the rubber industry for binding arbitration. (The NJIC is a standing body composed of equal numbers of
representatives of the industry's employers and trade unions.)
Pending the outcome of the arbitration, management agreed to pay
the 'X' builders at a fixed rate in return for a minimum level of
output.

The panel findings and the aftermath
On 17 May the NJIC panel met to consider the disputed rate. Both
the company and the union (the convenor) made submissions to the
panel. On the same day the panel found substantially in management's favor. At this point the story is taken up by a management
memorandum from which the following chronology was compiled.

17 May   The NJIC panel meets to consider the piecework rate and
          performance level. It finds as follows: 'In accordance
          with the terms of reference, the panel finds the appro-
          priate rate of production is ... at a price of....'
18 May   The convenor and the tire room steward report the panel's
          findings to the 'X' builders. The panel's decision is
          published by means of an Industrial Relations News Bulle-
          tin.
20 May   The convenor, his deputy (the branch secretary), and the
          tire room steward note (i.e., accept) the rate promulgated
          by the panel. (In the normal case only the appropriate
          steward notes agreed rates.)
23 May   (First shift) The new rate is applied by builders on the
          first shift.

	(Second shift) The 'X' builders on the second shift refuse to accept the panel's finding and adopt a policy of restricting output on the machines. The other builders follow suit.
24 May	The company issues a further bulletin saying that it 'anticipates that all tyre builders will honour the Agreement and honour the commitment made by the 'X' type builders to accept the findings of the NJIC panel and resume normal working.'
23-27 May	Other groups of workers stage stoppages or slowdowns to protest loss of earnings caused by tirebuilders' restriction of output.
25 May	As required by the company/union agreements, the company give notice of their intention to cancel the guaranteed week. After period of notice has expired the company will be entitled to lay off employees idled by the tirebuilders' action.
31 May	An extraordinary session of the works council is convened. Management memorandum notes: 'Problem not between Union and Company. The problem exists between the Union and its Membership.'
1 June	The company writes to the union's District and Regional full-time officials 'stressing need for support for Union Representatives [within the plant].'
4-12 June	Vacation
18 June	Tirebuilders meet with convenor and other branch officers (40 per cent attendance). They reject a request that they resume normal working and reiterate their demand for a better rate.
23 June	The convenor 'personally' hands the 'X' builders a letter from the union's Regional Secretary urging acceptance of the panel's finding. (This letter is quoted in full below.) The company notifies the convenor of its intention to start disciplinary procedure against the 'X' builders should they not accept the panel's decision.
26 June	A regular branch meeting is held. The union's District Official and less than one per cent of the branch membership attend.
27 June	Supervisors give the 'X' builders 24 hours' notice of intended disciplinary action and brief 'all hourly paid' employees on the situation.
28 June	Disciplinary action is deferred at the request of the branch officers in order to permit a mass meeting of the tire room the next day.
29 June	A mass meeting of the tire room (75 per cent of builders in attendance) votes to retain restriction on the output of the 'X' machines and passes a vote of no confidence in the tire room shop steward. Anticipating the vote, the steward has resigned. At the meeting the 'X' builders indicate that they are ready to accept the panel's decision. The company issues 'Official Recorded Warning' (i.e., penultimate warning before suspension) to the 'X' builders.

The convenor writes a letter to all tire room employees suggesting that once the 'X' builders accept the panel's decision a working party be formed to look into tire room grievances. Supervisors again brief all hourly employees.

30 June   The company communicates in writing with all the tire-builders regarding the possibility of a working party.
The company issues 'Final Recorded Warning' (final notice before suspension) to 'X' builders.

A two-shift meeting of the tire room releases the 'X' builders from their obligation to restrict output. Bye-election is held for new tire room shop steward. Platform of eventual winner is 'return to normal working and the formation of a working party.'

1 July   A 'full discussion' with the newly elected shop steward fails to gain immediate resumption of normal working.
The shop steward meets with the Factory Personnel Manager and the Production Director.

3 July   The new shop steward addresses a meeting of the tire room (50 per cent attendance) and obtains a resumption of normal working and an acceptance of the company's offer to set up a working party.

However, management's victory was a Pyrrhic one: apart from the legacy of bitterness left by the dispute, six months later the output of the 'X' machines was still being restricted, though nowhere near as drastically as at the height of the crisis. On this occasion, however, the 'X' builders' motives were different. They did not want to scandalize their colleagues by excessively high earnings from the rate they had all fought so hard to improve.

Before leaving the 'X' machine case, it will be useful to review briefly the positions taken by the workers and their representatives in the course of the dispute.

The tirebuilders

It will have been remarked that in successive meetings the tire-builders had backed the hard line of their colleagues on the 'X' machines. Although it was a shift of the 'X' builders who initially rejected the panel's findings (an earlier shift having worked the rate) the remaining 'X' builders promptly fell into line. The tire-builders as a group then made the fight their own, and in due course their militancy had outstripped that of the 'X' builders themselves. By 29 June the 'X' builders (no doubt influenced by the prospect of disciplinary steps against themselves) declared themselves ready to accept the rate. Only when suspension was imminent did a meeting of the tire room release the 'X' builders from the obligation to limit output.

Later chapters will be concerned with elucidating the reasons for the militancy in the tire room and in the factory in general. For the present certain consequences of the seniority system in the tire room should be noted. It will be recalled that the tirebuilders had insisted that the 'X' machines be manned by the most senior build-ers. This was part of the practice, enforced by the builders and acquiesced in by management, whereby all machines were manned ac-cording to seniority, with the most recent generation of machines going to the builders with the greatest seniority, and so on. This

practice had nothing to do with any intrinsic superiority or desirability of the newer machines; it reflected the fact that the
newer machines permitted higher earnings since their piecerates had
been negotiated more recently than those for other machines. (This
is an aspect of the phenomenon of earnings creep that is looked at
in the next chapter.)

However, it is the role of the seniority system in raising the
general level of militancy in the tire room to which I want to draw
attention. The seniority system meant that negotiations over new
piecework rates usually pitted management against the most politically powerful group in the tire room, viz. the older builders. It
also meant that other builders in the department had a stake - if
only an indirect one - in the outcome of the negotiations since
they would themselves in due course graduate to the newer machines.

Other production workers
The information in the files was sketchy with respect to the reactions of other groups of workers to the dispute. Their earnings
suffered as a result of the disruption since the various guarantees
or fall-back payments fell far short of what they were accustomed to
make on piecework. The record shows that at least one group (the
tire room servicemen) staged a token stoppage in protest at the loss
of earnings; it appears that other groups imposed slowdowns or
other measures. From conversations with other workers, it was clear
that the tirebuilders' intransigence had poisoned relations with
other departments and it appeared that informal and unorganized
pressures were brought on them to settle the dispute. In one case
that came to my attention, a tirebuilder who had approached an
extruder crew with a request that they not run a particular tread
size (presumably the 'X' tread) was heatedly turned down. Nonetheless the anger stopped short of any organized reprisal; the dispute
appeared to be regarded as a matter internal to the tire room, and
other groups of workers limited their actions to demands that
management protect them from the resulting disruption.

Workplace labor representatives
Until very near the end of the dispute, the impetus for the opposition to the piecerate proposed by management had come from a
group of builders. None of these builders held a position at any
level in the system of labor representation in the English factory.
(One of the 'X' builders was an ex-shop steward who had been defeated by the incumbent; it is difficult to judge the role this
played in the political difficulties of the latter.)

If the backing for the dispute came from the shop floor, what
were the attitudes of the elected representatives of the tire room
and the production workforce? As we have seen, the dispute eventually cost the tire room shop steward his position; it also created
a lot of ill-will in the tire room towards the convenor/branch
chairman: some tirebuilders said that they had agreed to the
reference to the NJIC panel on the convenor's assurance that it
would find in their favor.

In practice, the convenor and the shop steward adopted broadly
the same position. At all times they endeavored to argue the builders' case concerning the piecerate; equally, they tried at all

times to keep the dispute 'within procedure.' When the 'X' builders
disregarded their advice and refused to work the rate for the prescribed trial period, they negotiated the compromise whereby the
rate was referred directly to the NJIC panel without passing through
the intervening stages of the agreed procedure. When the panel's
finding was published, the convenor and the branch secretary took
the unusual step of adding their signatures to that of the shop
steward on the rate sheet. The subsequent rejection of the panel's
decision thus amounted to open defiance of every level of formal
labor representation in the factory. In spite of this rebuff, the
convenor and the shop steward continued their shuttle diplomacy in
the hope of producing a settlement.

At no point did the convenor or the shop steward threaten the
'X' builders with any kind of sanction. They limited themselves to
moral pressure. It is true that this pressure should not be dis-
counted: the convenor's formidable rhetorical powers must have made
the 'X' builders' position a very uncomfortable one. Nevertheless
the decision on the rate effectively rested with the tirebuilders
themselves regardless of the provisions of the company/union agreement.

The national union
The 'X' machine dispute was unusual in that permanent (i.e., extra-
workplace) officials of the production workers' union became involved. (In a sense, of course, the union had been indirectly involved as soon as the matter went before the NJIC panel, since it
was represented on that body.) On 22 June the union's regional
secretary personally wrote to all the production workers in the
tire room. This letter is quoted in full because of the revealing
glimpse that it provides of the nature of the relationship between
the union's national organization and its membership on the shop
floor.

                                                      22 June 1977
    To: All members of ... Company tyre room - Department....
    Dear Colleague,
    NJIC Conciliation Panel award - 17th May 1977
    I am taking the unusual step of writing to you direct in con-
    nection with the above matter. I understand that, arising from
    the decision of the Conciliation Panel, you have reduced your
    output because of the feeling of opposition to the Panel's de-
    cision.
        The purpose of this letter is to point out the serious po-
    sition which arises from your action insofar as the good name of
    the Union is concerned. I have spoken at length with the Dis-
    trict Secretary, Brother ..., and with the Chairman of your
    Branch, Brother ..., and the technical position which emerges is
    that our Union on your behalf gave an undertaking that we would
    abide by the decision made by the Conciliation Panel. This is
    in accordance with the agreed procedures to which the Union is
    party, both locally and nationally.
        Having given our pledge we are now seriously embarrassed by
    your action, the effect of which must be well known to you, and
    in all the circumstances I write in the hope that you will re-
    consider your position and resume normal working. It will be

realized that the present actions in the Tyre Room are having
serious repercussions on the earnings of other members in the
factory.

It is regrettable that the Union now finds itself in a position where we are unable to support the actions of our members
in the Tyre Room. If the Management had refused to implement the
award of the Disputes Panel I assure you that without hesitation
our Union would be officially in dispute with the Company. We
must therefore, having given an undertaking to abide by the
award, resume normal working and preserve our future credibility
in making agreements on your behalf.
Yours fraternally,

Regional Secretary

The 'X' machine case: conclusion
In common with the other stoppages in the English factory, the 'X'
machine strike, as well as the pressures that accompanied it, was
what Turner et al. (1967, p.223) have called an 'unofficial-unof-
ficial' strike, one 'that is, which has not merely the normal quality that it is not approved by the official union hierarchy, but is
particularly not first approved by the shop stewards' leaders. In
the motor industry, at any rate, this type of dispute appears to be
becoming the norm.' In this case, as we have seen, the actions of
the tire room enjoyed only the uncertain support of the shop steward
and that ended after the panel's findings had been made public.
These points will form the subject of later chapters.

Labor relations in the German factory

In stark contrast to the situation in the English factory, the
German factory was entirely free of fractional bargaining. In fact,
only occasionally did incidents occur to ruffle the placid surface
of labor relations in the German factory. The case-histories of
three of those incidents are given here.

The incident that came closest to erupting into fractional bargaining occurred a few months before my fieldwork. It originated
in a grievance over earnings on the part of the workers in the
Banbury department. The work in this department - where raw rubber
(both synthetic and natural) is broken down and blended with
chemicals in large mixers - is among the dirtiest in the factory,
and over half the operators were Turks. The trouble arose when the
operators found that their earnings had fallen behind those in other
departments; but their sense of grievance was particularly inflamed
by the discovery that they were earning less than many of the women
band builders (whose job it was to assemble the steel belts that run
under the tire tread). It is unclear whether managers had allowed
the situation to fester or whether there was a spontaneous outburst.
In any case, it appears that for a while a work stoppage by the
department had been considered a real possibility by management.
The situation was grave enough for the personnel manager to visit
the department during a work-break. He was accompanied by the works
council chairman and the single Turkish councillor. In the ensuing
meeting the personnel manager announced that the department's pay-

ment system would be redesigned so as to permit earnings on a par
with those in the rest of the factory.

Certain points about this incident are worth noting. First, in
the view of both personnel manager and works council chairman, the
problem had been compounded by cultural factors. For the Turkish
workers more than for the Germans or Yugoslavs, they said, wages
involved considerations of status; and it was an especial humili-
ation to be earning less than women workers, some of whom were also
Turks. Furthermore, information about comparative earnings travel-
led very fast among the Turkish workers who constituted a tightly-
knit community outside the factory, often having common quarters.
A second point concerns the operation of the factory's incentive
payment systems. The rate of output of the Banbury department
could be affected only marginally by the operators; the operations
were machine-paced. Consequently, the operators had no opportunity
to improve their earnings by raising their level of output. By
contrast, earnings in the band room were highly responsive to increased effort; the machines were semi-automatic, and the operators
were on individual piecework. Finally, it is especially noteworthy,
since this was the German factory's closest brush with fractional
bargaining, that the issue of wage differentials between departments
was described by the works council chairman as the one with the
greatest potential for causing an eventual strike.

This opinion was shared by management, and the movement of
earnings from one department to another was carefully monitored in
the personnel department. These last two issues form the subject
of the next chapter.

The second incident arose out of an assault by one worker on another. A Turkish worker had stabbed a Yugoslav with a work implement, allegedly after he had been provoked by an obscene suggestion
regarding his mother that was calculated to be especially offensive
to a Moslem. The Yugoslav had been briefly hospitalized; the Turk
had been instantly dismissed. (He had also fled town, presumably
to escape criminal charges.) A day or two after the assault, the
personnel manager was informed by the works council chairman that
a delegation of Turkish workers wished to see him over the events.
The personnel manager agreed to receive the delegation, and one
hour later about twenty workers filed into the executive dining
room and quietly took their seats. In addition to the personnel
manager, the works council chairman and the Turkish councillor
(besides myself) were present. Through the Turkish councillor (who
did not assume the role of spokesman for the group) the delegation
told the personnel manager that while they had no quarrel with his
decision to dismiss the Turkish assailant, they felt that in the
interests of fairness the Yugoslav should also have been dismissed.
The personnel manager replied that insults such as the one allegedly
made by the Yugoslav worker were completely unacceptable and constituted sufficient grounds for dismissal. However, in this case, he
went on, there had been no witnesses to the remarks, and so he was
unable to take any action. The delegation should understand that
to dismiss the Yugoslav in such circumstances would simply invite
a reversal of the decision in the courts. There, to the best of my
knowledge, the matter ended. The delegation broke up and returned
to work in the same dignified and undemonstrative way in which it

had sat through the hearing. It was difficult to judge its reactions to the outcome of the meeting; it had failed to obtain
its announced objective; on the other hand it had mounted an im-
pressive display of concern whose message was not lost on management or works council.

The third incident was a disciplinary hearing concerning another
Turkish worker; in this case, a serviceman in the tire room. (I
was present at the hearing, but not at the events leading up to it.)
The job of the serviceman, it will be recalled, was to keep tirebuilders supplied with components (ply, treads, steel bands, beads,
etc.) which are assembled into the green (i.e., uncured) tire. On
the occasion in question, the serviceman had found himself responsible for servicing more than the usual number of builders (either
because another serviceman was absent and/or because of the assignment of builders disproportionately to his machines at the time).
He had fallen behind in his work, and some of the tirebuilders had
been idled by the break in the flow of components. When the
serviceman had failed to respond to their calls (a lighted red bulb
above the machine), the builders began to jeer and curse as he
hurried back and forth past them. This was all done in a spirit
of fun; however it is possible that one or more of them went too
far or that the supervisor showed himself unsympathetic to the
serviceman's plight. At any rate, whatever the catalyst, the
serviceman had eventually been goaded beyond endurance and he had
simply stopped working. Apparently neither his supervisor, nor his
departmental manager, nor his divisional manager had been able to
persuade him to resume his work, for a disciplinary hearing was con-
vened in the office of the labor relations manager. Present at the
hearing were the serviceman, his divisional manager, the chairman of
the works council, the Turkish councillor (in the familiar roles of
interpreter and counsellor), as well as the labor relations manager.
The last chaired the hearing and elicited the story related above.
In the course of the hearing, the serviceman complained that the
supervisor (who had been born and brought up in Yugoslavia, although
he was an ethnic German) had shown favoritism towards the builders,
most of whom were Yugoslavs. Once the facts of the case had been
established, the labor relations manager asked the serviceman
whether he understood that, under the law, a refusal to carry out
his work would make him liable to instant dismissal. This was con-
firmed by the works council chairman. The serviceman replied that
he was aware of the law. The labor relations manager then told him
that he was excused the rest of the shift but that if he did not
show up the next day and carry on working normally he would be considered to have dismissed himself. Evidently the serviceman did not
carry his protest any further, for he was at work when I began my
observation of the tire room a week later. However, management's
failure to find a way of balancing their workloads plainly remained
a source of frustration among the servicemen.

None of these incidents by itself was of great importance. They
have been described in order to convey the feel or texture of labor
relations in the German factory, and to indicate the seams where the
factory's social fabric would have been likely to part first had it
come under a great strain. All in all, it was striking how rare was
any group-based or organized action along English lines. When it

did occur, as in the case of the first two incidents, it was more likely to be on the basis of shared nationality than common function. For example, at no time did the servicemen collectively protest to the departmental or divisional manager concerning their work assignments. From these accounts, it is equally striking how, even at this level and in relation to everyday incidents, the law exerted an appreciable influence.

THE IMPACT OF DISORDER ON PRODUCTIVITY

Labor productivity in the German factory was more than half again as high as in the English factory. (See Appendix A for a statement of how this estimate was arrived at.) To what extent can this difference be attributed to the presence of endemic fractional bargaining in the English factory? It is, of course, in the nature of bargaining that each party tries to raise the cost to the other of not agreeing to its terms (or to increase the inducement to agree to them). In industry the bargaining power of workers derives from their ability to halt or disrupt production or to impede its efficient operation (for example, by refusing to adopt more efficient work practices). Whatever concrete form they take, then, all the sanctions employed in the course of fractional bargaining are bound to have a direct effect on productivity; and in a situation where fractional bargaining has reached the point that it had in the English factory, productivity may be seriously depressed. Production, in effect, becomes a hostage to the demands of different groups in the workplace. As we have seen, in the English factory these groups had resorted to a variety of sanctions in order to coerce management into settling on their terms. These sanctions had become so commonplace a feature of the English workplace that in many aspects of their work operators' compliance with management's expectations was becoming problematic. Virtually any managerial initiative could be expected to meet with their resistance; and in many areas agreements with the workers could not be depended upon to ensure their cooperation. In short the situation resembled the one described by one of the studies conducted for the Donovan Commission: 'In Britain there has now developed a form of workplace bargaining where the parties immediately involved have come to accept that sanctions ... are a part of the normal background against which day to day negotiations take place on the workshop floor' (McCarthy, 1966, p.25).
      Some of the practices inimical to the English factory's productivity were not conscious bargaining tactics; but even in such cases, as I shall endeavor to show, the practices tended to be by-products of endemic fractional bargaining.

Measuring the impact of fractional bargaining

Before we examine the effects of fractional bargaining, a methodological point needs to be made. Ideally the two factories' production records would have provided me with a bsis for estimating the impact of fractional bargaining. Each factory did, of course,

maintain detailed records: in the tire room, for example, production reports were submitted after each shift; these listed
for each builder the number of tires built, the code No(s). of
those tires, and the total hours worked; in turn the total hours
worked by each builder were analyzed into piecework and non-piecework hours. In theory, an examination of the causes of non-piecework hours might have permitted some tentative conclusions to be
drawn regarding the effects of fractional bargaining. The production reports, for example, discriminate between off-standard
working (because some condition, e.g., machine malfunction, rules
out piecework) and idle time (due to component shortages, machine
breakdown, etc., whose causes are identified in the reports).
   However, this approach was ruled out by two difficulties. The
first was that the official analyses of the causes of lost production were insufficiently detailed for our purposes. From the
vantage point of the tire room's records, it was impossible to tell
whether a shortage of beads, say, that had idled a builder for one
hour was the result of inefficiency on the part of a serviceman, an
error in the scheduling of production by the production control department, a slowdown in the bead room, or some other circumstance.
   Another difficulty relates to the reliability of the production
records. The records were not a neutral, objective account of production; they, of course, represented a socially-constructed definition of what had taken place rather than a replica of what had
actually happened. As such, they unavoidably reflected the norms
and power relations on the shop floor. One major source of distortions in the records was the fact that, in each factory, they
served as the basis for the computation of earnings. Accordingly
they were the subject of a constant tug-of-war between tirebuilders
and supervisors. As we shall see in the next chapter, in some departments in the English factory, management had virtually sur-
rendered control over the recording and reporting of production to
powerful work groups. (8)
   In practical terms the resulting problem was this. A natural
starting-point for explaining the lower output in the English tire
room is the question: what proportion of the builders' time was
productively employed in each tire room? A very rough answer might
have been provided by the respective figures for piecework hours as
a percentage of total hours. In the German tire room 80 per cent of
the tirebuilders' time was reportedly spent on piecework; in the
English tire room the corresponding figure was 57.5 per cent for
steel radial builders (for the others it was less than 45 per cent).
(9) But what interpretation can be placed on these figures? Do
they indicate that there are more frequent (and longer) machine
breakdowns and component delays? Or do they simply reflect the
greater success of the English builders at maximizing their reported
non-piecework time (and so inflating their earnings)?
   In the light of these difficulties, in what follows I have simply
identified the principal ways in which fractional bargaining affected productivity, without trying to assign arbitrary quantitative
values to the individual factors involved.

Stoppages and other disruptions

It might be imagined that it would be relatively easy to measure the impact of work stoppages in the English factory. In fact the diffi-culties are daunting. (10) Clearly it will not do to consider only the workers directly involved in the stoppage; it is only when the secondary or consequential disruptions are taken into account that one can begin to assess the true cost. Given the flow-line nature of the tire manufacturing process, such disruptions may spread quickly. As we have seen, within one day of the tire room strike over the 'X' affair the entire passenger tire plant had been idled. However, it is more difficult to judge the impact of the much more numerous lightning stoppages of a single shift's duration or less. The manufacturing process is no doubt flexible enough to absorb the shock of some of the shorter stoppages. A lot might depend on local circumstances: for example, if other departments have been running ahead of schedule they will feel the effects sooner. Any assessment is further complicated by the fact that the effects of a stoppage may be disproportionate to its length. For example, after an 8-hour stoppage by the tire room it may not be possible for work simply to resume where it had left off. In the meantime the bands may have dried out; in which case they will have to be painted with a solu-tion to restore their tackiness (without which they components of the tire will not adhere to one another). In short, it might take some time for all the effects of the dislocation to wear off. (11)

    For these reasons no hard estimate of the losses directly at-tributable to work stoppages is possible. At most some suggestive results can be obtained by comparing the analysis of stoppages (Table 4.1) with the production summaries in the English factory. One solution to the problem of estimating the impact of stoppages would have been to compare output in stoppage-free months with that in stoppage-affected months. Unfortunately there were too few of the former in 1977 to make such a procedure practicable. However, the production figures show that output in March (the month that witnessed the 'X' machine strike) was 33 per cent below the average for the other months in the first half of 1977. In the same month 8 out of 23 working days (i.e., 35 per cent) were lost as a result of the strike. If one assumes that this relationship (i.e., pro-duction lost is roughly proportionate to working days lost) remains constant through the year, and if one further assumes that the figure of 33 per cent does not seriously understate the loss of production due to the 'X' strike, then it is possible to hazard an estimate of the impact of the major stoppages in 1977. The three such stoppages (Nos 27, 42 and 44 in Table 4.1) would then have cost about 7 per cent of production. Even allowing for error, then, it is plain that stoppages per se did not contribute significantly to the disparity between the two factories' productivity levels.

    It is still more difficult to assess the effect of the steady hemorrhage of production as a result of the shorter stoppages and other forms of bargaining pressure. The following sections describe the consequences of fractional bargaining for various aspects of the operation of the English factory.

Resistance to new equipment and methods

Virtually any change in the English factory became a bargaining opportunity. (12) An outstanding example of this process is the 'X'
machine dispute, but even fairly trivial changes could be exploited
as bargaining counters to be traded for some concession. Sometimes
this could take a farcical turn: on one occasion a change in the
number by which a department was known prompted a demand for a pay
increase. On another occasion workers appear to have won an increase when their department was moved to another location in the
same building. The move was deemed to have entailed a 'change in
job content.' The knowledge that even a minor modification might
lead to another round of protracted negotiations obviously inhibited
many small improvements. (13)
    The innovations for which it was most difficult to gain ac-
ceptance were those that affected more than one group of workers.
Take for instance the fortunes of the machine monitor system. Each
machine in the tire room was equipped with a terminal which would
have made it possible for the builder to notify a control room of
component delays, mechanical or electrical faults, etc. at the push
of a button. The control room would then have put out a call for
the appropriate serviceman or engineer. This system had been
physically in place for at least two years, but it was not yet
operational. The reason for the delay was that the system had had
to run the gauntlet of at least three different groups of workers
in the tire room: the production workers - both builders and
servicemen -, the engineers, and the supervisors. In 1975 it had
been accepted, subject to certain safeguards, by the engineers;
after an initial rebuff agreement had been reached with the staff
and supervisory union in 1977; however, at the time of my field
work it was still awaiting acceptance by the production workers.
Each of the groups whose work would be affected by the proposed
system had an effective veto over it and each exploited this fact
in order to extract concessions from management.
    It must be understood that the resistance to the machine monitor
did not stem from any threat to job security or disturbance of
settled work habits that it was thought to entail. In fact the
system would have reduced down time from component delays and
machine repairs and so would have gone some of the way towards
answering the tirebuilders' complaint that they were losing piecework earnings because of excessive down time. The point is that
changes that were intrinsically desirable from the point of view
of a group of workers were as likely to be opposed as any others.
The desirability or otherwise of a proposed change was immaterial
since the change was not opposed in principle but purely for bargaining purposes. (14)

Labor flexibility

Another major contrast between the two factories was the flexibility
in the deployment of labor enjoyed by German management but denied
to its English counterpart. One particular instance is worth
singling out for its implications for productivity in the English
tire room.

From the account of the 'X' machine affair it will be recalled
that the English tirebuilders operated a strict seniority system
with regard to the manning of machines. One of the consequences
of this system was the tendency for builders to become wedded to
particular machines. How was production affected by these property
rights in individual machines?

This can best be assessed by comparing the situation with that
in the German tire room. German builders had not acquired property
rights in particular machines. At the start of a shift they had to
check the schedule to find which machines they had been assigned to.
English builders, by contrast, went directly to *their* machines. Another difference was that German management had the freedom to
transfer builders between machines in response to shifting production priorities. In the English factory, on the other hand, so
long as piecework was available on his own machine, a builder would
refuse to be moved to another one; in fact many builders were unwilling to work on other machines if their own were down. These
differences are reflected in the fact that in the course of one week
in the German tire room only 5 per cent of the builders worked exclusively on one machine, while in a (different) week in the English
tire room 80 per cent did so. (15) Finally, when transfers did
occur in the English tire room output fell drastically, perhaps by
as much as 50 per cent. In the German tire room output was barely
affected in such cases. (This difference is largely explained by
the fact that the Germans would remain on piecework, while the
English would demand and get fixed payments in the event of a
transfer.)

Why was this inflexibility a major factor in the lower productivity of the English tire room? It must be remembered that
radial tires have to meet very stringent technical standards. For
example, they are subject to requirements of internal balance that
are considerably more exacting than for the older crossply tires.
One consequence of this was that, in both factories, machines had
frequently to be taken out of service for small adjustments. Since
they could not resume normal building until a number of sample tires
had been built, cured, and successfully tested, the ensuing delays
could be considerable. In addition to these delays there were, of
course, other interruptions to production from component delays and
machine breakdowns. As a result every machine experienced down time
and in many cases it was prolonged. This was as true in the one
factory as in the other.

The difference between the two factories was this: the ease with
which management could redeploy labor in the German tire room meant
that machine down time did not necessarily entail builder down time.
In the German tire room extra machines had been set up and builders
were transferred to them in the event of machine breakdown, maintenance check, and so on. In the English tire room, on the other
hand, if a machine was out of service a builder was often left idle.
Because of the difficulties of transferring builders between
machines, moreover, English management had adopted the practice of
manning every machine. There was no point in having a pool of reserve machines if they would not be worked or would only be worked
at half their capacity.

This inflexibility had repercussions that went beyond the depart-

ment itself. After all, the limitations on management's right to
assign builders to machines in practice amounted to a restriction
on its ability to determine what the tire room produced. This in
turn made it more difficult for management to balance the inputs
and outputs of different departments. For example, the presses in
the curing department were set up to take particular tire sizes.
If green tires of the appropriate size were not available the
presses were made idle. In other words, the inflexibility hampered
management's ability to coordinate production with the inevitable
result that there was an increase in the non-productive time of
other departments.

At the time of my fieldwork a productivity deal was under discussion in the English tire room. This would have provided for
greater flexibility, within agreed limits, in machine transfers.
However, the prospects for a workable arrangement looked unpromis-
ing. The divergent attitudes of management and builders are apparent from a brief exchange during a meeting of the tire room
working party (set up, it will be recalled, in the wake of the 'X'
dispute). According to a delegate of the builders, 'the practice
has been that so long as the components are there the builder keeps
bashing away. He's not expected to give up potential earnings when
the ticket is there on his machine.' In reply, a manager stated his
objective: 'We want to be able to move a man off a machine to take
up slack elsewhere, say in case of absenteeism, subject to the
equalization of earnings potentials [across different machines].'
(16)

I have concentrated on only one example of the rigidity of the
deployment of labor in the English factory. (17) Some other cases
will be described in the next chapter. Before I leave the subject,
I should mention that in the German factory the formal limitations
on management's right to transfer workers were fairly strict. No
transfer (other than of a temporary nature) could take place without
the consent of the works council. Nonetheless transfers were more
common and evoked none of the bitter opposition that they met in the
English factory. As a result management enjoyed much greater freedom to match the labor force to the shifting requirements of production.

CONCLUSION

The practices that depressed the English factory's productivity were
symptoms of a general erosion of management's control over production under the pressure of endemic fractional bargaining. This
loss of control was not - and this point cannot be overemphasized -
the result of any conscious strategy on the part of the workforce
to oust management from the workplace and/or replace it with a
system of workers' control. (18) Nothing, in fact, could have been
farther from their intentions. The inroads into management's
authority and prerogatives were rather the outcome of the exigencies
of fractional bargaining. British labor has traditionally been
lukewarm if not downright hostile to the idea of workers' control;
as Mann (1973; pp.21-2) has observed, 'job control is viewed by
trade unions as something which can be exchanged periodically for

economic rewards;   typically workers will gain some shop-floor control informally, and indeed surreptitiously, and then formally sign
it away in union-management negotiations.' In other words, workers
wrest control of production away from management not for its own
sake, but as a means of increasing their bargaining leverage.   This,
at any rate, was the case in the English factory.

This is not to argue that every work practice that harmed productivity was a bargaining tactic; but virtually all of them, at
least indirectly, were the outcomes of fractional bargaining.   For
example, some practices appeared to have grown up, almost unnoticed,
as a consequence of the new-found strength of work groups deriving
from their quasi-permanent mobilization for bargaining purposes.
Other practices, as we shall see, had been adopted by work groups
in order to protect themselves against the consequences of runaway
fractional bargaining.

The self-perpetuating character of the disorder in the English
factory is a principal focus of attention in the remaining chapters.
In fractional bargaining, 'different groups in the works get different concessions at different times' (Flanders, 1970, p.169), and
a concession to any one group serves as a cue to other groups to
press their demands in a spiral of claims and counter-claims.

If the productivity differential between the English and German
factories is largely a consequence of the presence of endemic fractional bargaining in the former, then what are the sources of the
fractional bargaining in the English workplace? and what conditions
inhibit its emergence in the German workplace? To answer this
question we turn in the next chapter to a comparison of the processes by which earnings were determined in the two factories.

APPENDIX

The extent of disorder in British industry

How representative of British industry as a whole is the experience of the English factory? It is difficult to give a precise answer to this question. The essence of fractional bargaining, after all, is that it is fragmented, small-scale, and decentralized; as I have remarked, it often merges almost imperceptibly into normal work routines. Consequently its incidence in British industry is very difficult to measure.

One thing is certain: the official statistics of work stoppages are of no use in gauging its extent. First, the figures compiled by the Department of Employment relate only to work stoppages, i.e., they exclude forms of pressure short of actual suspensions of work. Moreover they deliberately ignore strikes lasting less than one day. (19) There are compelling practical reasons for this policy; but its result is that the statistics are incapable of providing an index of fractional bargaining. In view of the decentralization of collective bargaining in Britain, this omission largely drains the official statistics of any informativeness; they systematically overlook the forms of industrial conflict that have become the norm. (20)

However, there are some survey findings that shed light on how widespread fractional bargaining is. One survey, of 970 industrial relations officers conducted from November 1977 to January 1978 found that over the previous two years nearly one out of every two factories in Britain had had some form of industrial conflict - stoppages, overtime bans, go-slows, etc. - and nearly one third had experienced strikes. (21) Similar findings were obtained by Daniel: at a 'period (predominantly 1975) when the number of days lost by British industry through strikes was the lowest it had been since 1968,' he found that 40 per cent of the establishments he surveyed had experienced some form of sanction in the preceding 12 months. (22)

The qualitative evidence indicates that fractional bargaining is very common in Britain, although it may not normally reach the pitch that it had in the English factory. This was one of the principal findings of the Donovan Commission, and it is supported by numerous case studies before and since the Commission's report. Most of these studies care cited at other points in this book.

Chapter 5

THE PROCESS OF WAGE DETERMINATION IN THE TWO FACTORIES

From the record of stoppages in the English passenger tire plant (see Table 4.1), it is apparent that pay and pay-related questions were the principal focus of fractional bargaining. And although managers in both factories voiced the fear that money was losing its power to motivate workers, there was little evidence to bear this out. In fact, in both places pay remained a consuming, often obsessive, preoccupation; whether workers were working, arguing, or striking, the objective was generally the same: to protect or improve earnings. As we saw in chapter 1, in both Britain and Germany labor's orientation to work appears to be predominantly instrumental. (1) Therefore the processes by which earnings were determined in each factory are a natural starting-point for any attempt to understand why fractional bargaining was endemic in England but absent in Germany.

Before looking in detail at the operation of the two pay systems, I should mention two points. First, in neither factory was the general level of pay a source of discontent. In both cases the production workers' earnings were substantially higher than the average for the region and higher than the average for the industry. Second, essentially the same pay system was in place in each factory. It was company policy to extend piecework to as many operations as possible, and the great majority of production workers were on some form of output-based pay scheme. (2) Since a variety of processes are involved in tire manufacturing, the pay schemes varied more between different departments in the same factory than they did between factories. Consequently the differences that there were in practice between the two systems cannot be explained by differences in their basic design.

SETTING PIECE RATES

In each factory the pay system was extremely complex. Consequently, rather than try to provide a detailed account of the two systems, this chapter singles out for examination the way in which piecerates were determined in each factory. (3) It was on this point that the contrast between the systems was most marked; and it was at this

stage of the wage determination process that the pressures of workplace bargaining were most in evidence.

The setting of piecerates may be illustrated by reference to the
two factories' tire rooms. In both cases tirebuilders were on individual piecework. If we ignore for the moment various allowances
and supplements (e.g., for shiftworking) and payments for non-piecework time, this meant that each builder's pay for, say, a given
shift was computed by multiplying the number of tires he had built
during the shift by the appropriate piecerate. Since tires vary in
size and construction, a separate piecerate had to be fixed for each
model of tire. How were these rates arrived at in each tire room?

Up to a point the same procedures were followed in each case.
First, a standard time for the job (i.e., for building a particular
model of tire) was estimated by the Industrial Engineering department. This was done by time study or by extrapolation from existing
tires of comparable construction. Next, the standard time was
translated into a piecerate for the job by reference to the negotiated hourly base-rate for the occupational grade to which tirebuilders belonged. For example, if the standard time for the job
was estimated to be six minutes, its rate would be one-tenth of the
builders' hourly base-rate, i.e.,

$$\frac{6 \text{ minutes}}{60 \text{ minutes}} \times \text{base-rate.}$$

Since the standard time was supposed to correspond to the time (including relaxation allowance, etc.) that it would take an average
builder to do the job in question, the resulting piecerate should
have permitted the builder to earn his base-rate in return for a
'normal' performance.

However, whereas a rate arrived at by this process was almost
invariably accepted in the German factory, it was almost invariably
rejected in the English factory. In England the industrial engineers' estimate became the basis for a rate proposal by management
to the builder(s); in other words it became the opening bid in a
round of bargaining. Although the shop steward might have stayed
in close touch with the time study, he would in no way feel bound
by its results. In Germany, by contrast, the workers' representatives were more directly involved in the time study. In the tire
room, for example, the works council chairman personally checked
the times (while in office he had taken eighteen months' of formal
training in work study) in addition to discussing them with the
builders. According to him, there had been no disagreements with
the company over times. (4)

One contrast, in particular, illuminates the profoundly different
conceptions of the process of setting piecerates. Strictly speaking, it is inaccurate to talk of a rate (i.e., a price) being set
in the German factory; the object there was rather to agree on the
appropriate standard time for the job. In the English factory, on
the other hand, the discussion was conducted in terms of money
values, the object being to negotiate a price for the job. Strenuous efforts by management to get the issue re-defined as the technical one of estimating the standard time had not overcome this
tenacious tradition on the shop floor. As one builder put it in a
meeting of the tire room working party: 'At the end of the day the
argument is about money.' (5)

The tendency to bargain over rates in the English factory was reinforced by the decentralization of the rate-setting process. As we
saw in the discussion of the 'X' machine case, the effective
authority to accept or reject a rate, initially at least, rested
with the work group, i.e., with the workers who had a direct stake
in the outcome. (6)   In Germany this prerogative was vested by law
in a subcommittee of the works council - the piecework committee or
Akkordkommission - which had an interest in maintaining consistent
work standards that would forestall jealousies between different
groups of workers.

The different approaches to setting piecework values were un-
doubtedly influenced by factors outside the workplace. In Germany
trade unions have historically been fairly receptive to the techniques of work study; indeed the objective, 'scientific' nature of
these techniques was believed to hold out the prospect of protecting
the worker from arbitrary behavior by his employer by narrowing the
latter's discretion. The national work study organization (REFA)
includes both union and employer representatives (Schmiede and
Schudlich, 1976, pp.265,323,337); and it has succeeded in intro-
ducing 'a high degree of work study uniformity in Germany' (OECD,
1970, p.41). In Britain, on the other hand, the scientific pre-
tensions of work study are generally treated with some disdain.
Since work study has an irreducible subjective component it cannot
fundamentally alter what in the final analysis is a bargaining process. The remarks of one British social scientist are not untypi-
cal: according to Eldridge (1973, p.52), F.W.Taylor

> simply ignores the fact that no matter how accurately one can
> time a job, one is still involved in a bargain over its price.
> Conflicts of interest are certainly not eliminated by 'scien-
> tific' rate fixing.... For Taylor, however, any attempt to
> bargain over the impersonal 'objective' standard time, arrived
> at by accurate rate-fixing, was absurd.

In conclusion, the differing conceptions of the process of setting piecework values may be summarized by describing the different
conceptions of their role in the process held by the workers' representatives in each factory. In Germany the chairman of the works
council considered it to be his responsibility to verify that the
standard times had been arrived at professionally and were not
grossly inaccurate; the English shop steward, on the other hand,
saw his role as that of obtaining the best piecework price that the
market would bear. (7)

It is not my intention to enter into the controversy over the
scientific credentials of work study. For the purposes of this
study the important question is a different one: what were the
implications of the two systems for the conduct of labor relations?

'DEMORALIZATION' OF THE ENGLISH FACTORY'S PAY SYSTEM

As we saw in the last section, setting piecerates in the English
factory was a bargaining process. Consequently, piecerates came to
reflect not some measure, however imperfect, of effort, but rather
the accidents of bargaining strength at particular times. It is the
argument of the rest of this chapter that the endemic fractional

bargaining in the English factory was largely the response of groups of workers to the resulting anomalies and inequities in the factory's pay structure. In its turn, it will be shown, the fractional bargaining generated further distortions leading to stepped up fractional bargaining, and so on.

It is well known that incentive pay systems are susceptible to a process of deterioration to which Slichter et al. have given the generic name of 'demoralization.' (8) The English factory's pay system exhibited the symptoms of demoralization:

(i) Substantial inequities in earnings and effort. A mixture of both tight and loose standards is both cause and effect in perpetuating a multitude of grievances over standards and a distorted wage structure; (ii) a growing average incentive yield. ... This figure, of course, indicates only payment results and not a higher level of effort; (iii) a declining average level of effort.... Informal quotas are met [well within the full workday]; (iv) a high proportion of 'off-standard' payments and times (1960, p.497).

To begin with, let us consider how far the last three points apply to the English case. (ii) At a time when the tire room in the English factory was consistently failing to meet its ticket (production target) the piecework earnings of the steel radial tirebuilders were averaging 200 per cent of their official base rate. In the German factory the equivalent figure was 140 per cent. As we shall see, the English piecework earnings were inflated by the illicit 'condensation' of piecework hours and by the loosening of piecerates through bargaining. While it appears that the German standard times were fairly loose (for reasons I will return to later in this chapter), the higher earnings also reflect the German factory's higher productivity. (iii) It is obviously difficult for an outsider to estimate levels of effort. So far as I could judge, when the builders were working the actual pace of work was not very different. However, in the English factory the frequency and duration of interruptions were far greater. It was striking how many machines were silent as early as three quarters of an hour before the shift was over; and management had raised with the shop stewards the issue of the 'bad practice of machines lying idle at the end of the shift.' In the German factory, on the other hand, work started tapering off 15-20 minutes before shift-end. (iv) As we have seen, in the German tire room reported non-piecework hours accounted on average for 21 per cent of the work day; for English steel radial builders the corresponding figure was 42.5 per cent and for other builders it averaged over 50 per cent.

These estimates provide a rough measure of the demoralization of the pay system in the English factory. But in order to grasp its full extent we must turn to Slichter's first criterion, i.e., a distorted wage structure characterized by substantial inequities. In England these inequities or anomalies were broadly of three sorts. First, the differentials between groups of workers no longer reflected acknowledged differences in skill or effort. Second, potential earnings varied considerably from job to job because of inconsistent piecerates. Third, various payments for non-piecework time (i.e., fallback rates) had become grossly devalued in comparison with piecework earnings.

As a result pay came to be seen as unrelated to effort and as the product of the capricious workings of the pay system. The disruption of differentials bred considerable resentment on the shop floor and drove groups of workers to try to 'correct' them by unilateral action. (9) At the same time, the variations in piecerates and the devaluation of fallback rates meant that earnings were highly unstable as well.

The effect on earnings of the devaluation of fallback rates may be illustrated by some examples drawn from the tire room. A tire-builder idled by a machine breakdown was paid at a fixed fallback rate which averaged half of what he might have been expected to make on piecework; if he was unable to work piecework because of poor quality stock he stood to lose about 40 per cent of his potential earnings; and he might be taken off a perfectly good piecework job in order to build test tires for the Technical Service Division, in which case he would be 35 per cent worse off. To the injury of this loss of earnings was added the insult of knowing that, under a separate local agreement, the neighboring, and lower-status, band-builder was guaranteed 100 per cent of his piecework earnings for experimental work and 90 per cent when substandard materials ruled out piecework. Local agreements in some other departments had the same or similar provisions. What part had bargaining over piece-rates played in bringing about this state of affairs?

It was an unwritten rule in the English tire room that any new piecerate should permit the builders who would work it to make at least their current level of piecework earnings. (10) On the face of it, this rule seemed eminently fair. What it ignored, howeever, was that current earnings were inflated by what was known to the industrial engineers as the fiddle factor (of which more presently). The exact size of this factor was of course unknown; and anyway it could hardly have been allowed for in new piecerates. But ignoring it put management in the invidious position of rewarding past cheating by incorporating its gains in new rates, of 'consolidating the fiddle' into new rates, in the words of one manager. Ignoring it also meant that new rates were invariably looser than old ones, and therefore as new jobs replaced old ones average piecework earnings in the tire room drifted inexorably upwards. In the mean-time, however, fallback rates, being for the most part fixed payments, increased only within the strict limits of successive govern-ment pay policies.

The disparities between older and newer piecerates also led to considerable variations in potential earnings from job to job and, in consequence, highly unstable earnings. For example, the replace-ment of a steel radial by a fabric radial tire on his machine (a common occurrence) cost a builder on average 10-15 per cent of his earnings. Since most jobs lasted several months the loss involved could be quite severe.

Needless to say, these anomalies were like an open wound on the shop floor. In order to try to mitigate their effects, groups of workers were driven to attempt to gain control over the pay system or at least to modify its workings. (11) This was made easier by the fact that the daily injuries inflicted by the anomalies kept indignation running high and so maintained these groups in a state resembling permanent mobilization. Moreover, since the anomalies

had undermined the pay system's moral legitimacy, groups had no com-
punction about exploiting every opportunity to improve their own
conditions with total disregard for the wider implications of their
getting their way.

The immediate or proximate stimuli for the endemic fractional
bargaining in the English factory, then, were to be found in the
demoralization of its pay system. Grievances over the irrational
workings of that system provided the agenda for the continuous bargaining on the shop floor.

Breakdown of managerial control over pay and work

It is unlikely that any piecework system is much older than the ways
that are used to circumvent or manipulate it. Roy (1955) has atmos-
pherically described the stratagems used in the 'resistance to and
subversion of formally instituted managerial controls on production'
in an American factory. Nevertheless the extent of such manipula-
tions in the German factory was minor; in the English factory, on
the other hand, they had reached the point where there was a serious
breakdown of managerial control over pay and work.

In the English tire room this was especially apparent in the
reporting (booking) of time and, to a lesser extent, of pieces.
Most typically this involved the overstatement by builders of their
non-piecework time (e.g., time lost through mechanical breakdown,
component delays, etc.). This resulted in their being paid twice
for the same time: first, for the tires they had built during the
fictitious down time; and, second, a fallback payment for the same
time. This overstatement was made possible by the fact that builders were in any case subject to numerous interruptions which could
not all be verified by supervision. There were interruptions in the
German tire room as well, of course, but they had not reached the
critical mass that they had in England (and if they were serious
builders were automatically reassigned to other machines), and the
German builders were allowed two rest periods at fixed times while
in the English tire room the timing of breaks was left to the builders themselves. As a consequence, outside the rest periods it was
rare for one to come across a German builder who was not working
(incidentally, this posed problems for the would-be interviewer);
at any time of day in the English tire room, on the other hand, the
smoking areas would be crowded with tirebuilders. These differences
obviously made the task of German supervision much easier when it
came to assessing builders' down time.

In these circumstances the manipulation of reported times in the
English tire room was relatively risk-free, and tirebuilders made no
secret of the fact that it was almost universally practiced. It is
impossible to quantify its extent, but it will be recalled that non-
piecework time as a whole accounted for over 50 per cent of all reported time for tirebuilders in England, while the corresponding
figure in Germany was 21 per cent.

For an example of a complete debacle, however, we must turn to
another department. Little needs to be added to the following memorandum written by the manager of the department in question:

As previously announced, a 100% check was performed on ... crew.

... On this occasion a supervisor was stationed at both the head and booking belt. No objection was raised by the crew to this arrangement, unlike the reaction [to an earlier attempt].

From this check we were able to glean both a list of [units] booked and scrapped by code, order and quantity, and the precise order and quantity of set-ups. Photostat copies of the checks are attached, as are copies of the corresponding time sheet submitted by the [operator in charge].

Since all the crew were aware of the check taking place, it might have been reasonably expected that the order of booking work on the time sheet would match the results of the check. However, as can be seen, no attempt was made to hide a complete misapplication of rates from the start of the shift to the end. Codes were booked as having been run several times in small numbers instead of the long runs which actually took place. The order of the codes were rearranged to maximize the number of fictional compound changes, and 'push-outs' were booked where, clearly, no such operations were carried out.

The time sheet as submitted yielded [earnings of X] which is not generally considered excessive by today's levels. However, if the codes, quantities and changes had all been booked as per the check, i.e., as run, then the [earnings] would have been [substantially lower].

It is highly unlikely that any group of piecework operators would, today, work piecework in a proper manner for a pay structure which only yielded this amount. [I] have been subjected ... to repeated complaints about [these] piecework rates and there is little doubt that the crew concerned, probably in league with their colleagues on ... shifts, are by their blatant misuse of the rates, even when under 'audit,' seeking a confrontation on [this] issue.

There can be absolutely no doubt that the referring of the attached time sheet with a direction to correct will result in a stoppage wherein the Company will be forced either to:
1. Increase the ... piecework rates (which it clearly cannot do under present [Government pay] controls and which would yield further temptation for more misapplication in the future);
2. Publicly acknowledge that the rates are obsolete and allow the fraudulent bookings to continue;
                          or else
3. Introduce a totally new pay system, as envisaged, but under the pressure of an industrial dispute and the likelihood of the system being costlier to sell.

In the event, management decided that it had no choice but to live with the existing practices while attempting to negotiate a new pay system for the crews involved. But the introduction of a new system was obstructed by the ruins of the old one. Nine months later management's proposals were no nearer acceptance. As the writer of the memorandum had presciently forecast, the crews simply were not ready to surrender the gains they had made by stealth and in which management had acquiesced, except on terms management considered prohibitive. During my fieldwork a check on one day's production had disclosed that, in addition to misbooking times and changes, the crews had claimed 33 per cent more units than had ac-

tually been produced. This discovery drew the following reaction
from a senior production manager:
  Subject: Stealing by Misbooking of [units]

  The production records from ... to ... show that pay for ... not
  produced was stolen from the company
                    [Calculation of Loss]
  This ... loss equates to ... per hour. Further, I must wonder
  what your supervision was doing during this time.
    I hear complaints from supervision that the operators get more
  than they do. When they permit the operators to steal 25.7% of
  ... reported plus whatever else, then they have no grounds for
  complaint.
    I expect you, your department manager, shift foreman, and
  supervisors to put a halt to this practice of outright falsifi-
  cation of production. You will be expected to show results
  starting 7 a.m., Monday....
    This letter is to be discussed with all your management people
  so that they understand what you expect of them.
Winking at some abuses, for compelling reasons to be sure, had invited others. (12)
  From the original memorandum it is clear that the crew's motivation in systematically falsifying the production records was to
prevent their own earnings sinking below a level commonly acknowledged as fair; however they had been so successful that their
earnings became the envy of the rest of the plant. In this case,
then, as in many others, the demoralization of the factory's pay
system had provoked workers into trying to take it over in order to
protect themselves from its effects; and, in taking the system
over, they completed another cycle in its demoralization.
  Many other practices in the English factory can be understood in
this light. Consider, for example, the resistance shown by the
English workers to transfers. This can largely be explained by the
disparities in potential earnings from one job to another. (13) As
we have seen, because of such disparities tirebuilders were strongly
opposed to allowing management a free hand in moving them between
machines; the seniority system in the tire room represented a way
of allocating jobs in accordance with the power relations and conceptions of equity in the department. In another department a work
stoppage (No.30 in Table 4.1) resulted when crew members were reassigned following an equipment shortage. The problem was that the
operators were assigned to different duties at different pay levels;
they struck claiming that the same payment should be made to all. A
final example concerns a 'Machine and Labour Utilization Study' that
was aborted when the crew involved threatened to go out on strike.
Firm-wide manning comparisons had suggested that the English crew
was overmanned. As a result, management had ordered an industrial
engineering study of the operation in order to determine if any manpower savings could be made. However, the crew objected to the
study and told management that 'if we proceeded to take a study on
the mill line then the crew would withdraw their labour.' Eventually the production managers vetoed the study saying that 'the feelings of the ... crew were running high and under no circumstances
would they permit the I.E. study to take place. The crew had indi-

cated that should an attempt to take a study be made then they would
walk out immediately and would not stop to close down the mills.'
Two and a half years earlier another crew had been run down and the
surplus operators had apparently been offered alternative employment
at lesser rates of pay or redundancy. According to the crew, the
forgone earnings of those who had accepted other employment were
substantial. A recent request that their rate be re-appraised had
been turned down by management on the grounds that 'there had been
no change in the job or work content and as such, under current
Government wage restraint, no adjustment could be made.' If that
was so, the crew told management, then 'there has been no change in
job or work content and therefore no manning reduction study is
justified.' (14)

Other endogenous sources of demoralization in incentive pay systems

Bargaining over piecerates was not, of course, the only reason for
the demoralization of the English factory's pay system. Other factors were at work as well and are present to a greater or lesser
degree in all incentive pay systems. The senior industrial engineer
in the German factory kept on file a memorandum listing the more important of these factors. They were: (15)
   1 The operators' experience and skill are constantly improving.
      [The so-called learning curve.]
   2 It may not be possible to establish fixed work methods because
      of variations in the condition of the material. The rubber
      industry is particularly subject to this problem.
   3 Methods prescribed by Technical Services Division may not be
      applied consistently.
   4 Quality control instructions may not always be followed.
   5 It may not be possible to adjust rates to reflect small im-
      provements in equipment and layout.
   6 Non-piecework time may be overstated.
   7 Over time the quality of components may improve so that pro-
      cedures at later stages of production become unnecessary.
These factors resulted in wage drift or earnings creep, that is to
say the tendency for actual earnings to outstrip negotiated rates.
The phenomenon was evident in both factories. It will be recalled
that the earnings of German tirebuilders were running at about 140
per cent of the negotiated level.
   Wage drift tends to undermine a pay structure not because it
raises earnings, but because it does so unevenly. (16) For example,
some operations, being machine-paced, offer relatively little opportunity for the operator to increase his earnings through greater
effort or dexterity. As we remarked earlier, this was the case in
the Banbury department. The same is true of opportunities for cutting corners (in Roy's phrase, 'streamlining the job'). One particular shortcut, used in both tire rooms, alone shortened the time
for building the average tire by 5 per cent. For safety reasons,
however, it was not an approved procedure and thus was not reflected
in the standard times for the jobs it affected. In addition, small
technical improvements and refinements of work methods not adjusted
for in the rates occurred unevenly; as one would expect, they

tended to be concentrated in departments where the equipment was relatively new and untried. As the result of these factors, and others like them, the extent of earnings drift varied from operation to operation and from department to department, thus disturbing established differentials in the workplace.

In both factories this built-in instability was aggravated by the coexistence of a wide range of different processes. The consequence was a proliferation of different pay schemes, each tailored to the requirements of a particular department or work group, and each with a different potential for drift. However, since these tendencies were present in the German system as well, they are not sufficient to explain the demoralization of the English pay system. (As we have seen, the blame for that rests principally with the practice of bargaining over rates.) However, in the English case, the effects of these endogenous factors were far more damaging, for reasons that are examined in the next section.

External factors in the demoralization of the English pay system

A number of other factors, this time originating outside the workplace, contributed to the demoralization of the English factory's pay system; these were inflation, incomes policy, and productivity bargaining. First, during the three years 1974-76 the consumer price index in the United Kingdom rose by 68 per cent; in Germany over the same period it rose by 19 per cent. Second, starting in November 1972 wage increases had been limited by a succession of government incomes policies. (See Table 5.1; there was a brief period of relatively free collective bargaining in 1974-75.) Third, starting on 1 August 1977, the Labour Government relaxed the terms of the incomes policy to permit increases in excess of the pay norm where they were paid for by changes in the work methods of the workers involved (under productivity deals).

The effect of the British rate of inflation was, of course, to generate powerful pressures on the shop floor for compensating increases in earnings. The successive incomes policies were intended to dam up these pressures; instead they diverted them along alternative, unofficial, channels. It was this last development that most helped to undermine the English factory's pay system.

Incentive payment systems pose special problems for an incomes policy. Clearly earnings cannot be fixed without removing their incentive effect. Accordingly, British governments tried, instead, to regulate incentive earnings by prohibiting changes in the systems themselves, and in their components, i.e., in base rates, piecerates, and fallback payments. (17) In this fashion, while provision was made for individual earnings to vary, no overall increase should have resulted (except in the unlikely event of a general increase in effort).

However, this left piecerates for new jobs to be freely negotiated. (Strictly speaking it left only the standard times to be mutually agreed while freezing the base rates; however, for reasons discussed earlier, this distinction had no practical effect on the shop floor.) Consequently new piecerates became the focus of shopfloor pressures to protect earnings from inflation. (18) The dis-

TABLE 5.1   UK Incomes Policies 1972-77

Date	Norm for wage increase	Special features
November 1972- March 1973	Stage 1 - six-month freeze	
April 1973- October 1973	Stage 2 - £1 + 4 per cent	
November 1973- July 1974	Stage 3 - £2.25 or 7 per cent (whichever greater) + 1 per cent for anomalies	Broken by miners' strike. Threshold payments linked to price increases. (Eventual total: £4.40.)
September 1974- July 1975	Social Contract	TUC agree unions should limit wage demands to increases in cost of living.
August 1975- July 1976	Phase 1 - £6 per week limit on earnings	Introduced with sup- port of TUC.
August 1976- July 1977	Phase 2 - 5 per cent limit within range of £2.50-£4.00 per week	Supported by TUC.
August 1977- July 1978	Phase 3 - 10 per cent on earnings	Self-financing pro- ductivity deals per- mitted in excess of 10 per cent limit. TUC withdrew support for limit.

Note: In March 1974 a Labour government succeeded a Conservative
one.

tortions to the pay structure from this source were compounded by
the uncontrolled effects of the inherent tendencies to disorganiza-
tion that we looked at in the last section. The incomes policies
could not check piecework earnings drift but they could and did
oblige management and the shop steward body to look on helplessly
at the consequent unravelling of the pay structure. (19)
     As a result, five years of incomes policy had weakened all formal
authority in the workplace. They had reduced annual negotiations to
a purely ritualistic exercise whose outcome had been decreed in advance and elsewhere. Still more damaging, they had prevented the
shop stewards from collectively taking the initiative in correcting
the growing anomalies in the pay system. Since these anomalies
simply would not await the repeatedly deferred return of free collective bargaining for their correction work groups took the law
into their own hands. Management offered strong resistance, but as
anomalies proliferated and shopfloor pressure grew this position
became untenable. In order to alleviate some of the grosser inequities or to appease the more aggressive work groups management found

itself compelled to make piecemeal concessions. Typically these
concessions were small and of limited scope, such as higher fallback
rates for specified circumstances outside the control of a work
group. In one case, for example, a crew obtained a higher payment
for time they were idle because of modifications to their machine,
but the amount still fell far short of their forgone piecework
earnings. All the same, management found that it was difficult to
prevent a tactical withdrawal from turning into a rout. The piecemeal correction of anomalies only threw into relief other anomalies
or even created new ones. And it became known that, pay policy or
no pay policy, if pushed hard enough by a group of workers management would give in. One way in which management tried to contain
the resulting contagion of claims was by obtaining promises that
concessions would not be used as a springboard for further claims.
A typical clause in one agreement read as follows: 'This agreement
has no precedent value and will not be recognized as a basis for
negotiation by any other group.' However, since this undertaking
was generally given by the shop steward representing the group that
had secured the concession, it is not surprising that other groups
did not feel bound by it. Perhaps more important, formulas of this
sort simply failed to come to grips with the underlying reality.
This was that each new concession, regardless of the formal under-
takings accompanying it, heightened expectations in the factory that
individual work groups could obtain redress for their grievances by
their own actions.

   These concessions breached the letter of the incomes policies.
But isolated concessions made at this level could escape the vigi-
lance of the Department of Employment in a way that factory-wide
concessions could not. For example, management refused to agree
to a general revaluation of fallback rates in the tire room although
it had granted increases in individual cases of hardship. The tire
room shop steward pointed out that, in granting these increases,
management had already violated the incomes policy; therefore they
could not hide behind that policy to deny an across-the-board revaluation. Management replied that the difference was that 'we can
hide one-off deals.' Consequently, one of the legacies of the incomes policies was to shift the scene of effective bargaining from
the factory level to the individual work group. This stimulated the
habit of independent action by groups of workers and made it very
difficult for the shop steward body to develop and implement any
concerted policies.

   In other words, incomes policy was undermining the authority of
labor representation in the English factory in just the same way as
it had earlier contributed to the weakening of the authority of
trade unions and employers' associations. Earlier, incomes policies
had hastened the flight from industry-wide collective bargaining because agreements at that level were too large and too public to
escape the government's attention. Now the government's attempts
to hold factory agreements within its pay guidelines were diverting
powerful bargaining pressures into fractional bargaining on the shop
floor. (20)

Productivity bargaining

The third external factor contributing to the demoralization of the
English factory's pay system was productivity bargaining. As I have
mentioned, the third stage of the Labour Government's 'counterin-
flation policy' permitted pay increases above the norm provided that
they were financed out of the proceeds from increased productivity.
As a result, beginning in August 1977, separate groups of workers
presented their demands in the form of 'self-financing productivity
deals.'

In the short term the restored flexibility brought some tangible
relief. For example, it enabled management to obtain the long-
delayed acceptance by supervision of the machine monitor system.
It is difficult to be categorical about the longer-term effects,
but certain points seem to stand out. First, productivity bargaining was a spur to make-work practices. And second, it intensified
the disorder in the factory pay structure.

Productivity bargaining had the perverse effect of stimulating
the growth of make-work practices because it put a price-tag on
them. Once the custom became established of buying changes in work
practices, it became virtually impossible to make any change without
first paying for it. The saga of the introduction of the machine
monitor system may again be referred to in order to illustrate the
paralysis that might result. By providing an objective record of
machine down time this system might have taken much of the heat out
of supervisors' relations with tirebuilders. Nevertheless supervision blocked its introduction for two years after its acceptance
by the engineers. The reason for this was that the engineers had
received an inducement for agreeing to implement the system; but
before supervision could receive their inducement the first stage
of the Labour Government's incomes policy had intervened. Consequently the system remained in limbo until government policy permitted a pay increase as part of a productivity deal.

The practice of productivity bargaining, then, must bear a large
share of the blame for the rigidity of labor in the English factory.
It encouraged the cultivation and hoarding of make-work practices
for eventual sale; it led to a legalistic resistance to any duties
not spelled out in a worker's job description; and this in turn
fostered a parochial and fragmented view of production.

In addition, productivity bargaining contributed directly to the
demoralization of the factory's pay structure. It did this by
awarding pay increases to groups of workers within the factory with
little or no regard to considerations of equity. In theory productivity bargaining was supposed to compensate workers for extra
effort or for disturbance to their work habits and to enable them
to share in the benefits from technological change in the workplace.
In fact it simply distributed windfall gains to those groups whose
production methods happened to be changing most rapidly; and in the
same process it distorted the differentials between groups.

Self-defeating consequences of fractional bargaining

We have already noted the paradox that the pay system's demoralization was in large part the outcome of the actions of groups trying
to protect themselves from its effects. The weakening of management
authority under the pressure of fractional bargaining led to other
frustrations and irritations for the workforce as well. While it
was intact, management's authority had provided a basis for the integration of the activities in the workplace and for the stability
of pay and work relationships. The weakness of management had meant
the weakness of that coordination as well. Brown has put the point
well: 'The control of individual jobs by workers when they do not
also have control of the broader coordination of those jobs can lead
to situations that are very unsatisfactory from their point of view'
(1973, p.153).
    Six months before my fieldwork a meeting of the passenger tire
plant's production workers had been held 'to determine what was
going wrong in the [plant].' In the course of that meeting, according to a statement issued following it, 'a motion of no confidence in Management was carried by an overwhelming majority.' The
statement continued:
    Criticism was expressed of various aspects of both Management and
    Representation. It is our belief, however, that there is a
    genuine desire by most employees to get back to a period of
    stability which will enable us to produce more tyres, upon which
    everyone's livelihood ultimately depends. To this end it was
    further resolved that we introduce a cooling-off period and give
    [shop stewards] twenty working days to sort out the problems [in
    the plant]....
At the suggestion of the shop stewards, the meeting had drawn up a
list of some forty criticisms to be submitted to management. Among
the points relating to the tire room were the following:
    1. Improved scheduling - lack of coordination between tyre room
        and stock preparation.
    3. Reduction of engineering delays by early notification of
        changes.
    4. More changes to be implemented at weekends.
    5. Standardization of machines to create more flexibility.
   11. Inadequate coverage of three shifts by Technical Division.
What is striking about many of these criticisms is that they are directed at management's failure to manage effectively. A recurring
point is the failure to ensure a smooth flow of production: for the
tirebuilders this meant the absence of a steady flow of components
from the stock preparation departments; and for the workers in the
curing department, in turn, it meant the tire room's failure to keep
the presses supplied with the right sizes and types of green tires.
    If this solicitude about essentially managerial problems appears
surprising, it must be recalled that delays and interruptions entailed lost piecework earnings. For the most part, as we have seen,
these complaints were complaints about the consequences of the workers' own actions. The coordination of production was hampered by
the inflexibility of labor and by the absence of reliable data for
scheduling purposes. (22) If more machine changes were to be implemented at weekends, then more machine setters would have to be per-

suaded to come into the plant over weekends. Again, if there was to
be full coverage of all three shifts by the Technical Division, more
personnel from that division would have to work shifts. By implication, then, management was being criticized for not taking a
tougher line with other groups of workers. (23)

Another complaint voiced at the meeting concerned management's
slowness in resolving grievances raised by the shop floor. In particular, the apparent abdication of responsibility on the part of
junior and middle management was singled out for criticism. 'It is
our belief,' the statement recorded, 'that all problems should be
solved quickly and as close to the source as possible. To this end
Divisional and Departmental Management should be given a clear
mandate and should have authority commensurate with their responsibility.' The strength of feeling on this point is illustrated by an
outburst at a meeting of the English factory's works council. One
shop steward said: '[The plant manager] appeared to be placing all
the blame on the shop floor; he suggested he should take a look at
the Management where they sit on the fence and do not make decisions
over the simplest of matters.' (24)

However, given the disorder of the factory's pay system, it is
doubtful if even the best designed procedure could have supported
the weight of the resulting grievances. (25) There was another way
in which the demoralization of the pay system had increased the
delays in processing grievances. Although management accepted - or
at any rate paid lip service to - the principle of settling grievances as close to their source as possible, in practice it found this
position untenable. Instead, in order to minimize the risk of
supervision or junior management unwittingly setting precedents
that might be exploited by other work groups, management found
itself compelled to centralize decision-making. As the authority
to make decisions became more centralized, the point of decision
became more remote from the shop floor and the delays in resolving
grievances became longer. Since junior management either would not
or could not commit itself, very few grievances were resolved in the
early stages of the agreed procedure. Consequently the procedure
itself came to be seen as protracted and time-wasting, and the
earlier stages were short-circuited or the procedure was ignored altogether in favor of some form of unconstitutional action.

Another shopfloor complaint concerned 'delays in implementing
piecework rates when differentials are already established.' The
absence of a piecerate on a job, of course, generally meant that the
possibility of piecework earnings was denied to the builder. This
could be especially frustrating for the builder when it involved
well-known quantities, for instance a tire switched from one type of
machine to another. Since the performance characteristics of each
type of machine were known to the industrial engineering department,
so the criticism ran, it should have been possible to extrapolate a
new rate by applying the differential between the machines. As the
minutes of a working party meeting recorded:

[The convenor of shop stewards] stated that machine differentials
had been established in the past, [so he] failed to understand
why Industrial Engineering had to study a tyre that had an established rate because it was building on a different type machine.
This creates loss of earnings and loss of production.

What this criticism failed to allow for, however, was the effect of piecework bargaining on the structure of piecerates in the English tire room. This insistence on bargaining over individual rates had led to a crazy quilt of piecerates with little or no internal consistency. Consequently, setting a new piecerate could not be a matter of simply cranking one out by applying pre-established differentials.

Piecework bargaining led to delays for other reasons as well. First, the endemic confrontations over rates meant that the industrial engineering department was always fully stretched. There was a constant traffic of aggrieved shop stewards and operators in and out of the office. Second, there were further delays because even the most innocuous-appearing rates had to undergo a thorough screening before being proposed to the shop floor. Again piecework bargaining was largely to blame. Management's caution was understandable, because the consequences of an error could prove dear: once a rate had been adopted it was practically irrevocable; and a loose rate might not merely distort the rate structure further but could be used as a lever to drive up new rates. (26)

The German factory presented a complete contrast. The main differences in the approaches to establishing piecerates have already been outlined; the effects of these differences were quite dramatic. In the German industrial engineering office work proceeded at a calm, unhurried pace in an atmosphere far removed from the state of siege in the English office. The German tire room's rate structure formed an integrated whole while the English tire room's was a piecemeal accumulation of the outcomes of trials of strength. In the German tire room several standard times had been reduced (with the agreement of the works council chairman) following the speeding up of certain automatic machine cycles; such a step would have been unthinkable in the English factory. The result was that in Germany, once the initial program of time study was complete, new tire sizes and models could be introduced into the pre-existing framework of rates like new elements into the periodic table; and if errors were discovered they could be corrected without upsetting a precarious truce in the workplace. In England, on the other hand, and in spite of management's efforts to move towards the German system, each minor variation - an additional component, a slightly revised building sequence - might require returning to square one.

The habit of independent action by separate groups in the workplace also imposed other, more direct, costs on the workforce. As we have seen, the flow-line nature of the manufacturing process meant that a stoppage or delay at any point might slow down or even shut down production and lead to a loss of piecework earnings; in more serious cases it might result in lay-offs.

Not surprisingly, then, each group of workers attempted to insulate itself from the effects of its neighbors' actions. This trend was evident in the growing incidence of a phenomenon, noted by Turner et al. (1967, p.55) in the British automobile industry, of 'workers striking against having their work interrupted by strikes.' In 1976 the entire passenger tire plant had struck in support of a demand for guaranteed earnings for a period when production had been disrupted by a work-to-rule by the engineers. (27) As a result of this strike management had conceded the principle of 'pay guarantees

when normal working is not possible because of industrial action by
other groups of employees ... not party to the ... Agreement.' (It
will be recalled that both engineers and supervisors belonged to
different unions and were therefore covered by their own agreements.)

By the time of my fieldwork there were increasing signs of agita-
tion to get these guarantees extended to cover disruptions by other
production workers as well, i.e., by members of their own union.
Table 4.1 lists a number of such cases. For example, on one occasion the tire room servicemen stopped work to demand compensation
for loss of earnings due to the restriction of output by the tirebuilders in connection with the 'X' case (No.33). On 25 October
1977 according to management's records, 'the cementhouse claim
guaranteed earnings when any group including their own union members
are in dispute.' And as a result of the four-day stoppage in October 1977 (No.42), a tirebuilder had begun a test case in the courts
in order to obtain unemployment benefits for the period that he was
laid off.

In these circumstances, relations between groups of workers and
between unions inevitably came under great strain. When payment of
one week's wages was delayed by a work-to-rule of punch-card operators (belonging to the staff and supervisory union) there was a
storm of protest from production workers. Another incident, this
time in the truck tire plant, provides a vivid illustration of the
problems that might flow from the weakening of management's authority. The account is drawn entirely from management files.

[A] stoppage of work occurred [in the curing department] 8 p.m.
2nd shift yesterday. All operators in this department left the
company premises. Mr ..., Union Representative [i.e., shop
steward], who was on the shift, objected to the claimed disruptive practices by the paint and line crew [in the tire room]
which prevented green tyres reaching [his department's storage
area]. Paint and line crew stopped work at 6:50 p.m. to clear
cement tanks due to blocked lines. It took 30 minutes to clear,
[they] recommenced work, and then [the] crew stopped for un-
scheduled break for further period.

Mr ... objected to the additional break period. [He] held a
departmental meeting and the decision was to go home. [From file
dated November 25, 1977.]

[The two shop stewards and the convenor were called to the
office of the Factory Personnel Manager. The company informed
them that it had started an investigation and was considering
disciplinary action. November 28, 1977.]

Suspension letters issued to Mr ..., Union Representative, and
four other operators.... One week's delay in application of suspension to allow appeal. [The convenor] requested meeting with
Factory Personnel Manager. Remaining 52 operators who walked out
given final warning letters ... [November 29, 1977].

Operators will not be available on an overtime basis to cover
the suspended operators, therefore ... curing will cease during
3rd shift which will effectively reduce [truck tire plant] output
by 50% [December 5, 1977].

In ways like these the custom of independent action by individual
groups of workers entailed consequences that were self-defeating

from their point of view. Far from enlarging the freedom of each
group, this custom - since it was claimed and practiced by everyone
- only increased the disorder in its environment and so led to repeated frustrations.

CONCLUSION

In concluding its generally negative study of the operation of incentive pay systems in British industry, the Prices and Incomes
Board (NBPI, 1968, p.98) said:
> We have ... found considerable disenchantment among workers with
> the constant time-consuming process of shop-floor haggling, in-
> equity, falsification of work records, inversion of customary
> differentials and lack of security, which are so often associated
> with conventional PBR systems.... Our investigations have shown
> that workers are as concerned with the equity and stability of
> earnings as they are with their absolute amount.

Plainly, however, these are not generic problems of incentive pay
systems (at least at this level of intensity); they are, rather,
a product of certain distinctive attributes of British labor relations, which may be loosely grouped under the heading of breakdown
or fragmentation of government. In the next chapter we will look at
the reactions to the endemic fractional bargaining in the English
factory of various groups endowed with formal authority in the workplace, i.e., supervision and shop stewards.

Chapter 6

BREAKDOWN OF GOVERNMENT IN THE WORKPLACE

If fractional bargaining involves a breakdown or fragmentation of government in the workplace, then how did the groups possessing formal authority in the English factory react to it? Why were they unable to bring it under control, or to channel or integrate it? Again the answer largely takes a circular form: fractional bargaining engendered conditions that undermined the very structures that might have held it in check. This chapter traces the ways in which fractional bargaining had spread disaffection among supervision and indicates how, in turn, this had weakened management's control over pay and work; it then goes on to show how the capacity of the factory's labor organization to integrate sectional interests among the workforce had been eroded under the continuous pressure of fractional bargaining.

SUPERVISION

In the last chapter we saw that one reason for the breakdown of management control over pay and work in the English factory was the failure of supervision to police them effectively. This failure was part of a pattern of disaffection in the ranks of supervision stemming from developments in the workplace which had undermined the supervisor's status, pay and function. Other signs of this disaffection were the unionization of supervision, (1) stoppages, and other forms of pressure on management. What factors were responsible for this disaffection?

It is well known that various trends have stripped the foreman of many of his traditional functions and of much of his authority. One of the earliest statements of this process is Roethlisberger's (1945). He reported that foremen had come to see themselves as the 'stepchildren' of industry. The foreman had to 'operate under a set of technical conditions, social relations, and logical abstractions far different from those which existed 25 years ago' (p.284).

> Under modern conditions ... there seems to be always somebody in
> the organization in a staff capacity who is supposed to know more
> than he does.... For some time he has not been able to hire and
> fire and set production standards. And now he cannot even trans-

fer employees, adjust the wage inequalities of his men, promote
deserving men, develop better machines, methods and processes,
or plan the work of his department, with anything approaching
complete freedom of action. All these matters for which he is
completely or partially responsible have now become involved
with other persons and groups, or they have become matters of
company policy and union agreement. He is hedged in on all
sides with cost standards, production standards, quality
standards, standard methods and procedures, specifications,
rules, regulations, policies, laws, contracts, and agreements;
and most of them are formulated without his participation (ibid.,
p.285).

However, by themselves, these trends are insufficient to explain the
disaffection of the English supervision; for they have been no less
marked in German industry than in British. (2)

Therefore the reasons for the disaffection must be looked for in
circumstances peculiar to the English factory. And among those circumstances it is the endemic fractional bargaining that appears to
be most clearly implicated. First, as we saw in the last chapter,
fractional bargaining had led management to centralize decision-
making (i.e., away from supervision) in an attempt to minimize inconsistencies that might be exploited by strong work groups to
obtain equivalent terms. As the pressure for consistent policies
grew, the level at which decisions were reached was irresistibly
pushed higher in the chain of command. (3)

Second, decision-making was increasingly becoming a process of
bargaining between management and shopfloor representatives. Consequently, the shop steward, sometimes joined by other operators co-
opted on to working parties, was in almost continuous contact with
middle management. For example, over a period of five weeks, the
tire room shop steward worked on average less than three hours
piecework per week (according to the production records). As a
result, supervisors often learnt of decisions after the production
workers. (4) These developments reflected the displacement of the
formal lines of authority in the workplace by a new set of power
relations. If management wanted to maintain production it had no
choice but to come to terms with the work group and its representatives.

Nonetheless it was the supervisors who had to bear the brunt of
the production workers' anger at the operation of the pay system.
When they braved this anger and took a stand they were not unlikely
to find themselves undercut later by concessions by management. One
incident reveals the depth of feeling on this point. In order to
try to tighten control of the booking of times, management had proposed to introduce a 'time audit stamp.' This stamp on a tire
report would have signified that it had been verified by the appropriate supervisor. The staff and supervisory union informed management that its

members cannot agree to use the time audit stamps until certain
written guarantees are given by management ... [including]
management backing when ... items ... are queried by the process
workers, [and the assurance that] should any time sheet or cards
be signed and approved by a Production Supervisor and subsequent-
ly a query raised, then there will be no adjustment or correction

other than by the individual who originally approved the time
[and] after consultation on the problem.
There was certainly justification for complaints by supervision on
this score. As a result the supervisor found himself caught between
the anger of the shop floor and the uncertain support of management;
in these circumstances he was not inclined to challenge operators'
reports of their times.

To make matters worse, over the past few years supervision had
witnessed a steady erosion of the differential between their pay and
that of the production workers, as a combined result of fractional
bargaining and incomes policy. (5) According to a management study
of April 1977 the margin then stood at 3 per cent. Inevitably this
meant that in some departments a large minority of production workers earned more than the average supervisor.

It is not surprising then that supervision generally felt aggrieved at their lot. This view, moreover, was not confined to
them: almost unanimously tirebuilders said that they had no interest in promotion. The supervisory ranks were kept filled largely by
back injuries and dermatitis.

Largely in self-defense and out of a feeling that management had
deserted them, supervision had turned to the tactics of the shop
floor. Ten years earlier an attempt by the staff section of the
production workers' union to organize supervision had failed. But
since then another union - catering exclusively for white-collar
workers - had successfully recruited the whole of supervision. From
the start this union had pursued a militant policy, staging at least
one official strike and numerous other actions. (6) In Germany only
a very small proportion of supervisors and white-collar workers were
union members. Nevertheless, irrespective of union membership their
pay and conditions were negotiated by the chemical workers' union,
with the result that their pay was advanced more or less proportion-
ately with that of the other workers. This forestalled any leap-
frogging or competition between supervisors and production workers.
As might be expected under a piecework system, however, many operators had higher earnings than their supervisors; without exception
the tire room supervisors considered the physical effort involved in
tirebuilding to justify this situation. (7)

The unionization of English supervision was only a symptom of a
more profound transformation in the making, with lasting and pervasive implications for the operation of the factory. This was the
transformation of supervision from an arm of management into another
group of claimants in the workplace. This tendency was well advanced by the time of my fieldwork. It took the form of a creeping
paralysis of the supervisory function as supervisors refused to
assume responsibilities not spelled out in their job descriptions
and opposed all changes not accompanied by pay increases. Of course
these positions were tactical and so, in theory, reversible. But
what had started out as a bargaining tactic seemed to be in the process of hardening into habit. And the more these tactics were seen
to bring results, the more they were cultivated.

The English factory's management was aware of these trends and
had introduced a program of measures designed to turn the tide by
'reaffirming the role of supervision as the first line of management.' This program included setting up a joint working party to

develop recommendations; institutionalizing consultation through a
monthly joint council; arranging supervisional conferences away
from the factory; improving supervisional training; ensuring that
supervisors were promptly briefed on agreements with the production
workers' union affecting their departments; generally improving
communications with management; improving physical facilities;
and so on. Management also undertook to correct the differential
between supervisors' and production workers' pay.

It was too early to judge whether these reforms were bearing
fruit or were regarded as mostly cosmetic measures that left the
real problems untouched. (8) The sentiment seemed to be widespread
among supervisors that they would be happy to see management put
their union out of business by itself taking on the responsibility
of safeguarding their interests. For example, an officer of the
union told me that he would welcome a fixed percentage link between
supervisory and production workers' pay (incomes policy permitting).
Nevertheless it seems unlikely that enhanced financial guarantees
could have done more than sugar the pill of the supervisor's loss
of authority to militant groups of workers.

LABOR REPRESENTATION

In the circumstances of the English factory, loss of managerial
authority did not lead to a corresponding increase in the authority
of the shop stewards. In fact, fractional bargaining weakened all
formal authority in the workplace - including that of labor representation. In addition to examining the effects of fractional bargaining on different levels of labor representation in the English
factory, the rest of this chapter introduces the final concern of
this study, which is to elucidate the attributes of British labor
relations predisposing them to disorder. The disorder in the
English factory, it has been shown, was the product of the competitive pursuit of sectional interests by different groups of workers
in the workplace - what I have referred to as fractional bargaining.
This raises the question, why was labor representation in the
English factory powerless to stem this disintegration of its
authority? The answer, it will be suggested, lies in certain
structural features of the factory's labor organization; and these
features, in turn, derive from the structure of labor relations in
Britain.

Inter-union relations

The fact that each class of workers in the English factory (production workers, engineers, and supervisory and staff personnel) was
organized by a different union (9) and had its own representative
machinery was, as already remarked, a source of inflexibility in
work assignments; it was also a source of wage and status competition among the workforce.

Each class of workers constituted a bargaining unit which conducted separate negotiations with management; and since each had
an agreement with a different renewal date, there were few times

of year that were entirely free of negotiations or the maneuvering
that generally led up to them. There were also signs that, with the
increased flexibility permitted under Phase 3 of the incomes policy,
negotiations might become very protracted affairs. In 1977 the
negotiations between the company and the supervisory union had been
due to be completed by April 1; instead they had remained dead-
locked until the start of Phase 3 in August. Another consequence
was that negotiations were conducted with an eye on the terms most
recently won by the other workers and the bargaining postures that
they seemed likely to adopt. In these conditions jealousies were
never far from the surface. The two-week withdrawal of cooperation
by supervision in September 1977 had been precipitated by a long-
overdue settlement in the engineers' negotiations, apparently on
terms more generous than those on offer to supervision. Thus militancy was given a sharper edge by the need of each set of negotiators to be seen to be obtaining a settlement at least as favorable
as the other groups'. (10)

Cooperation between the representatives on other matters appeared
to be only rudimentary. An officer of the supervisory union said
that there were 'no real relations' between his union and the engineers; the two were 'on speaking terms only.' While there was a
'working relationship' with the representation of the production
workers, there was 'no love lost' between them and the supervisors.
It was generally agreed that any attempt to form a common works
council would be blocked by the engineers. Both other groups of
workers expressed resentment at the airs that, they said, the engineers gave themselves. In 1975 a resolution had been passed at a
branch meeting of the supervisory union stating that 'Production
Supervision would only report machine faults to their counterparts,
Engineering Supervision, as opposed to hourly-paid Tradesmen.' (11)

It should be added that management appeared to look on these
divisions as a blessing. On its initiative, the three company-union
agreements included clauses stating that each union 'will act independently of any other Union.'

However, this study was focused principally on production workers, and it is to the relations within that group of workers that I
now turn.

Relations between branch and membership

We have seen that the fractional bargaining in the English factory
was fuelled by constant comparisons of earnings between different
groups of workers. According to the branch secretary, the issue of
relativities between departments and work groups was the main problem facing the factory. If it was to be remedied, he said, there
was a clear need for shop stewards to 'coordinate their rate-
bargaining' in order to prevent the growth of further distortions
in the factory's pay structure. But this presented a dilemma, for
the steward's function was to get the best possible terms for his
district.

It will be recalled from chapter 3 that there were four senior
stewards (making up the branch's executive committee) who were
elected by the production workforce as a whole. Of these the

branch chairman (convenor of shop stewards) and his deputy, the branch secretary, deserve special mention. To what extent were these representatives, who were free of sectional ties, able to provide a basis for the integration of the divergent interests among the production workers? (12) And, in particular, were they in a position to bring about any coordination of the rate-bargaining in the English factory?

As the account of the 'X' case showed, the influence of these officials - whom I will refer to as the branch - in local matters was very limited. Over a wide range of issues it was usual for shop stewards to conduct their own negotiations without so much as keeping the branch informed of their progress. On one occasion, for example, the branch chairman had to contact management in order to learn the tire room's reaction to a proposed productivity deal. When the branch became involved, it tended to be after the event and in the role of mediator between management and workers. The fact is that such authority as the branch had over its membership was, to put it kindly, moral or social in nature. Or, as two sympathetic observers have said, 'As surveys show, [British] trade union leadership is consent leadership, which works by persuasion and argument.' (13)

The branch's limited authority had imparted an element of make-believe to its negotiations with the company. (14) Many of the more important terms of the company-union agreement were being violated almost before the ink was dry. For example, the agreement contained the following provisions:
- 'No demands will be made by any individual or groups of individuals during the life of this agreement.'
- 'No industrial action shall take place ... whilst [a dispute] is in procedure.'
- In the case of a stoppage, 'the Company and the Union shall not consider the merits of the dispute ... until the interruption has been terminated.'

As we have seen, these provisions were routinely disregarded, as were others concerning the procedures for setting piece rates, the payment of wages by bank transfer, transfers of employees between departments, and so on.

What were the branch's powers over its membership? In the course of one set of annual negotiations, management asked the branch if it was prepared to apply sanctions in cases where its members breached the agreement. According to the minutes, the branch replied that 'it would continue to play its role in honouring the agreement.... A branch could discipline an individual under certain conditions. The facilities are available for this, but there has never been any necessity to take action.' This answer was, of course, an evasion, but it more or less accurately stated the official position. Constitutionally the branch was empowered to discipline members. In extreme cases it might withdraw their union cards, which would be tantamount to dismissal under the closed shop agreement with the company. In practice, however, these powers had long since fallen into disuse, if indeed they had ever been live options.

What is true is that, short of sanctions or direct instructions, the branch used every effort to ensure that its members stayed within the terms of the agreement. The branch (qua branch) did try

to keep grievances within the agreed procedure; it initiated no
fresh demands during the lifetime of an agreement; and, when
stoppages took place, the branch entered into discussions with
management only at the latter's request. If part of its membership
staged a stoppage, the branch's response normally followed the lines
already familiar from the 'X' case. First, it tried to gain a
return to work while the grievance was being handled by the agreed
machinery. Second, so long as members remained in breach of procedure, they were denied the branch's backing. Third, if invited to
do so by management, the branch used its good offices to try to
bring about a settlement. However, the branch accepted no responsibility for policing the agreement; it was left entirely up to
management to make use of the disciplinary powers at its disposal.
Although the branch did not challenge the company's right to discipline employees, it nevertheless represented them in disciplinary
hearings. Finally, if management conceded a pay increase beyond the
terms of the agreement, the branch would not oppose it. (15)

What were the practical effects of this abstinence on the part of
the branch? Essentially it acknowledged the de facto autonomy of
the work group. Usually it made little difference to the outcome of
a dispute whether branch backing was given or not. For, as Kuhn
(1960, p.99) has pointed out, 'some groups have more strength to enforce *their* demands than the whole union has to enforce its demands.' As we saw, a stoppage by any one department could idle the
passenger tire plant almost as quickly as a factory-wide stoppage
would have. Accordingly branch support, with the implied threat of
a factory-wide strike, did not materially enhance a group's bargaining power; conversely the denial of that support was not a credible
deterrent to action by the group.

Before leaving the question of the branch's capacity to integrate
the sectional interests among the production workers, I should point
out that the branch's apparent weakness was in no way a reflection
of any internal political weakness on the part of the branch officials. The branch chairman had been in office for twenty years, and
all four officials were re-elected in a heavy poll (70 per cent)
shortly after the conclusion of the fieldwork. The opposite is
closer to the truth; such influence as the branch had conserved was
attributable to the political and intellectual capacities of the in-
cumbents, rather than to the constitutional powers of the office.
(16)

Can it be said, then, that the fractional bargaining in the
English factory was caused by the branch's failure to ensure - by
the use of sanctions if necessary - that its membership respected
the company-union agreement? In a trivial sense, it probably can.
But it was not that the branch was unwilling to discipline its
membership; it was rather that it was unable to do so. The branch
secretary told me that the branch 'should be in a position to discipline people who hurt the members' interests. But the membership
tends to support the underdog. It's a complete and utter waste of
time to try to discipline anyone. I've had a lot of abuse thrown at
me [when I've tried to do it].' The interesting question, therefore, is: what factors prevented the branch from asserting its
authority over its membership? And for the answer, I think, one
must look at the structure of British labor relations. (17) That
subject is covered in the next (and last) chapter.

Relations between shop stewards

It has been noted by Brown (1973, p.146) that 'in matters of wages;
an integrated shop steward body is a force for stability.' What
mechanisms existed in the English factory for integrating the activities of the shop stewards?

The principal official organ for this purpose was the branch committee. As we saw in chapter 3, this committee brought together
both the senior stewards/branch officials, who were elected factory-
wide, and the shop stewards, who represented separate districts.
The object of this hybrid arrangement was to coordinate policy
within the factory. In practice the committee formulated the
branch's claim in the annual negotiations; but otherwise it only
rarely, if at all, functioned as a unified entity. Instead each
shop steward handled the issues arising in his district in isolation
from his colleagues and without regard to their potential plant-wide
implications.

Even if the branch committee did not try to regulate the behavior
of individual shop stewards, did it not at least provide a forum
where some measure of socialization into a less parochial perspective took place, or where some sense of shared problems was imparted, that counteracted the pull of constituency? Again, on the
evidence of the persistent sectionalism in the English factory, the
answer has to be no. There was no indication of any attempt by the
shop stewards to concert their actions or to work out a collective
solution to the problems that afflicted them all (for example, by
collectively defining the appropriate differentials between different groups of workers, and then pressing management to adopt a new
rate structure embodying these differentials).

The relations between the shop stewards appeared to range from
indifferent to bad. We saw in the last chapter how an unofficial
break taken by one department had led to a walkout by another. The
tire room steward said that his proposals for cooperation had drawn
no response from his colleagues. Branch committee meetings, he
said, generally broke up in disagreement, and there was 'bad blood'
between some of the stewards. (18)

However, the shop stewards' failure to coordinate their bargaining cannot be understood in terms of their attitudes or personali-
ties. In fact there was unanimity among the stewards with whom I
talked that the main irritant in the factory was 'inconsistencies
between groups and departments.' They were also unanimous in de-
ploring the tendency for earnings to be determined by 'industrial
muscle.' The tire room steward, in particular, was emphatic about
the need to replace the patchwork of 'parochial deals' in the
English factory by comprehensive agreements. The factory's 'pay
structure is worse than British Leyland,' he complained.

These opinions notwithstanding, when it came to negotiations in
the tire room the steward insisted on raising the question of fallback rates although it was the subject of discussions on a factory-
wide basis. When I taxed him with the possibility that his insistence on separate arrangements regarding fallback rates might
help perpetuate the inconsistencies that he deplored, he explained
that he was in principle opposed to parochial deals; but, he said,
'that's the situation.' No shop steward could afford to postpone

his own district's claims while other groups of workers were obtaining improvements. (19)   In other words, the reasons for the
stewards' failure to coordinate their bargaining are to be found in
the logic of the situation that confronted each steward.   'However
great the parties' sense of social responsibility they cannot afford
to lose their place in the race.   Their behaviour, in other words,
is not freely chosen;   it is structured by the conditions in which
they operate' (Flanders, 1970, p.165).   In the English factory the
demoralization of the pay system had unleashed such intense
pressures on the shop floor that the shop steward had to be seen
to be pressing his district's case regardless of the wider consequences of doing so.   It is to an examination of the pressures on
the shop steward that we turn in the following section.

Work group pressures on shop stewards

The Donovan Commission found that 'it is often wide of the mark to
describe shop stewards as "trouble-makers."   Trouble is thrust upon
them.   In circumstances of this kind they may be striving to bring
some order into a chaotic situation, and management may rely heavily
on their efforts to do so' (1968, pp.28-9).   What sorts of pressures
shaped shop stewards' behavior in the English factory?
     It should be made clear that a work group, in the sense that the
term has been employed in these pages, is not coextensive with a
shop steward's district;   each district contained a variety of different work groups.   It is also important to stress that it is a
mistake to try to reify the work group: most work groups did not
have stable identities in the English factory;   instead they formed
and re-formed around specific issues.   They were, in short, essentially narrow interest-based coalitions of workers founded on
transient common goals rather than on lasting personal ties.   A
tirebuilder's participation in a work group, for example, would
depend on whether a particular development affected him as a passenger tire plant worker, as a tire room operator, as a tirebuilder, or
as a radial tirebuilder, and so on.   (I have earlier referred to the
permanent mobilization of work groups in the English factory;   it
would perhaps be more accurate to talk of the permanent availability
for mobilization of the English workers.)
     It follows that shop stewards must be seen as
     leaders of complexes or coalitions of work groups.... Individual
     groups may act on their own, perhaps contrary to the advice of
     their steward and the wishes of other groups within his constitu-
     ency, or all the groups may act together under his leadership,
     while for other purposes many work groups may coalesce behind a
     committee of stewards, or even contrary to the wishes of the
     stewards' committee (Clegg, 1970, pp.24-5).
One of the shop steward's main tasks, then, was to balance and integrate the interests of different groups and latent groups in his
district.   This task was made difficult by the fact that the demoralization of the factory's pay system constantly threw up anomalies that created dissensions and jealousies within the district.
The steward could assure the unity of his constituency only by re-
storing some semblance of equity to the pay relationships within it

and with other groups of workers outside it. Hence it became
politically imperative for him to try to secure a degree of control
over the operation of the pay system. What I am describing is of
course the dynamic of fractional bargaining. (20)

The political sensitivity for the shop steward of the issue of
pay relations between groups of workers in his district can be
gauged from the following exchanges in the course of a meeting of
the tire room working party. Management had proposed a productivity
deal that would have established a new (and substantially higher)
base rate for all tirebuilders. It would also have involved wiping
the slate clean of all existing piecerates; in their place a new
internally consistent rate structure would have been introduced.
However, this would have required an entirely fresh program of time
studies. The tire room delegates had welcomed the proposal but they
were apprehensive about the mechanics of its implementation. Specifically they were troubled by the suggestion that each section in
the tire room (e.g., crossply builders, steel radial builders) would
have to be time-studied in turn rather than a start being made on
all of them simultaneously.

> Delegate: We want lots of activity; not only in crossply.
>   Some radials are just as bad. It's got to be seen
>   that you're dealing with all the anomalies.
> Manager A: You realize an overall approach will take longer?
> Manager B: (To manager A) Could we put an extra man in?
> Delegate: We want it seen that all of the anomalies are going
>   to be dealt with. You've got to think of the shop
>   floor reaction.

And later on in the same meeting:

> Delegate: There is one item we think will be a sore point: the
>   time study. We want movement on 2-ply and short
>   batch as well, so that the shop floor can see steps
>   are being taken. There are other groups we want to
>   have investigated. It's important that they be con-
>   cluded at the same time. We've got to have some-
>   thing, some program that looks and is comprehensive
>   on the sore points.

As we saw earlier, another consequence of the demoralization of
the pay system was instability of earnings. Its immediate causes
were the variations in earnings potentials from job to job and the
relative depreciation of the fallback rates at which builders were
paid when idled for any reason. In an earlier meeting of the
working party the tire room shop steward had called for 'a simpli-
fied method of payment.' 'We want established rates so that everyone knows where they are,' he said.

> Steward: We want stabilization of earnings. That will create
>   an atmosphere for the stability of production. We've
>   got to have [fair fallback rates] as protection.
>   What guarantees do you want that abuse won't occur?
>   We're not thinking about the past but about the
>   future. The main grievance is the instability of
>   earnings. It leads to overbooking and other abuses.
>   The question is, do you trust us or not?
> Manager: On present evidence, no.
> Steward: In return for a chance we will give you assurances.

```
Manager:      You've let us down on ... [mentions an experimental
              machine on which the operator was judged to have
              given a half-hearted effort in spite of being guaran-
              teed full earnings].
```

The intensity of the pressures to which shop stewards were subjected is also evoked by another exchange. Management had proposed
that the new rate structure be phased in over eighteen weeks. As
the time study of each section was concluded the new rates would
have been implemented. The tire room shop steward pressed for a
completion of the entire program of time study within eight weeks
and the simultaneous application of all the new rates at the end of
that period.

```
Steward:      Could you do a collective study in eight weeks?
Manager:      I'd have to look.
Steward:      Then we have a 'failure to agree.' (21)  I can't go
              on putting people off.  It's me that gets the kicks.
Manager:      I could promise twelve weeks.
Steward:      I can put it to the meeting.  But I'll anticipate the
              outcome by putting in a failure to agree.  An interim
              payment would have kept the lid on.  I'm not having
              the finger pointed at me and called a management
              lackey.
Manager:      [Amplifies the twelve-week offer.]
Steward:      In the meantime we'll have to buy this time.  I'll go
              ahead and register the failure to agree.
Manager:      Please hold off till Friday;  we'll get you a defi-
              nite answer by then.
Steward:      Get us the fallback rates and we'll hold the situ-
              ation.  If there's no answer by Friday night,
              there'll be a failure to agree.
Manager:      We can give you a statement of intent setting out the
              provisions that are proposed subject to [the opera-
              tors' acceptance of] the productivity items.
Operator
delegate:     We'd like a written statement for our meeting.
Manager:      We'd prefer the statement to be mutual.
Steward:      There must be some way to reduce the hardships.  So I
              won't have to wade through mounds of shortages [i.e.,
              claims for make-up money for excessive down time]
              with ... [the departmental manager].  Even then [all
              the operators get is ...].  All we've had is nega-
              tive, the runaround from [... another manager].  It's
              me who's been getting the kicks;  they're asking me,
              what did we put you in for?
Manager:      I sympathize with your position.  I'll get you a firm
              answer for your meeting.
Steward:      Then I'll withhold the failure to agree.
```

It is possible that some of this was staged for management's
benefit on the principle that 'the power of a negotiator often rests
on a manifest inability to make concessions and meet demands'
(Schelling, 1973, p.19). However, the views that the tire room shop
steward expressed in private and in meetings with his district did
not differ from what he had told management. For example, in the
course of the subsequent mass meeting where management's proposals

were discussed by the tire room the steward made a point of de-
nouncing what he calls attempts by some people on the shop floor
to undermine his position. When one questioner asked whether
management's assurances could be trusted, the shop steward rounded
on him; it was more a question of the shop floor needing to earn
his and management's trust, he said.

   Although new to the position, the tire room shop steward was a
seasoned trade unionist. He had been convenor of shop stewards in
another factory - and in another union. In conversations and interviews he contrasted his current frustrations with his previous experience. His present union was too democratic, he said; it was a
case of every man being his own shop steward. In particular he deplored the absence of any effective disciplinary procedures; without them hundreds of jobs might be put at risk by the actions of one
man. Their absence was hampering his efforts to restore fairness to
tire room earnings. Since he had been elected to serve out the rump
of his predecessor's term of office, much of his time had been taken
up with trying to 'quell rumors' on the shop floor. His task had
also been made difficult by what he termed the selfish motivation in
the department; in its place he was trying to gain acceptance of
the principle that, regardless of machine, they were all tirebuilders. But if equity was to be restored to the tire room, democracy
had to be tempered with discipline. At least once, having no official sanctions at his disposal, the steward had considered using
unofficial ones: on that occasion he told me that he was thinking
of instructing the tire room servicemen to black (i.e., to refuse to
service) the machines of certain 'radicals' in the department. (22)
At the time of my fieldwork he was doubtful about being a candidate
in the regular elections which were then only a few months away. In
the event he ran and was returned unopposed.

   The views reproduced here, if not their forthrightness, were not
peculiar to the tire room shop steward. For example, his neighbor
condemned the 'tire room situation of every man for himself.' He
made it plain that he tolerated no independent action in his district. There was room for only one steward, he said.

   The dilemma faced by every shop steward was that of reconciling
the consequences of the piecemeal negotiation of piecerates with the
need to secure equity in the distribution of earnings in his district. To renounce the right to press for the best rate that
management would concede would have been utterly foreign to him.
After all, the shop steward's very raison d'être in the British
workplace lies principally in his role as a piecework bargainer.
But, as we have seen, the shop steward's own inclinations in the
matter were largely irrelevant anyway. Shopfloor pressures left him
no choice but to fight every rate to the final bell; the appearance
of not doing so (as in the case of the tire room shop steward's
predecessor) could well prove politically fatal.

   Nevertheless the anarchic pay relations that resulted posed
almost as serious a threat to the shop steward. Not for the first
or last time there was an objective identity of interest between
management and the representatives of the workers. In the past,
management had performed the latent function for the shop steward of
maintaining an orderly pay structure by resisting demands that had
threatened to disrupt it. But now the erosion of management's

authority and the accompanying demoralization of the pay system had
destroyed that rampart and had left the shop steward exposed to the
full force of the jealousies and rivalries on the shop floor.

Some shop stewards did succeed in bringing a measure of stability
to their district's pay relations. It is instructive to look at how
this was done by the steward in a district neighboring the tire room
(the same steward who was quoted a few paragraphs earlier). The
steward in question was well established and had achieved a remarkable personal ascendancy over his district. The district contained
several distinct departments and sections so that the potential for
disruption was present. Furthermore, in two sections the rates were
very loose - in one case because the rate structure had been negotiated very recently and in the other because design changes had
sharply increased output while the rates remained unchanged. How
had the shop steward prevented these disparities from leading to
grossly different earnings? Quite simply he had restricted output
on the operations with loose rates so that their earnings had not
exceeded those from the operations with tighter rates. (In this he
had been aided by the fact that his district's earnings were the
highest in the passenger tire plant.) He had also skillfully traded
increases in the output from the loosely rated operations for increases in the earnings from the tightly rated operations. He told
me that his goal was 'to establish fair [pay] systems [in his dis-
trict].... The same effort, even pushing a broom, deserves the same
pay. I've tried to avoid the tire room situation of every man for
himself.' In this way the vagaries of the factory's demoralized pay
system had been held in check, but at the expense of output.

This shop steward did not hesitate to gain his point by calling a
stoppage when it seemed tactically expedient; in fact there were
six stoppages in his district in the course of 1977. In contrast to
those in the tire room, however, these stoppages had not escalated
out of control and taken on a life of their own. None of them had
exceeded twenty-four hours. Apparently these tactics had worked;
we have noted that his district's earnings were the highest in the
plant. But they had not simply had the result of wringing concessions out of management; they had also had the effect of pre-
empting any incipient discontent in the ranks. 'Although on the
whole the stewards ... appear as attempting to minimize trouble ...
when trouble seems inevitable, they attempt to assert their leadership in order to maintain their authority over the operatives.' (23)

Although it was clear that management felt this steward was a
thorn in their flesh, it was equally apparent that the advantages of
a strong steward were not lost on them. It was no accident that,
when a dispute arose in a neighboring district (not the tire room)
whose shop steward was in hospital, management had turned to this
steward. His intervention appears to have led to a settlement of
the dispute and a prompt resumption of work. Far from fearing a
powerful shop steward and a united district, management welcomed
them. In the course of annual negotiations, management had complained to the union side 'that, when Membership elects a Representative, that person did not appear to be given the opportunity
to do the job and did not have any support to go with it.'

CONCLUSION

As this account has shown, there had been a loss of authority at every level of labor representation in the English factory. Instead power resided with shifting coalitions of workers on the shop floor. Why had this process taken place in the English factory? And why had the German factory been immune to it? These questions are examined in the next chapter.

Chapter 7

CONCLUSION

'People outside do not understand how angry the men feel about
this. The trouble has been going on unresolved for years. The
boilermakers have become an elite for no other reason than that
in the past they shouted the loudest. It is now our turn.' An
outfitter at the Swan Hunter shipyeard to a (London) 'Times'
correspondent (3 December 1977).

'We've been over to Europe. They're no better than us, but the
they're more reliable and regimented. [It is something to do
with] the attitudes of our society today, [we've] abandoned responsibility. This doesn't make an iota of difference to the
workforce. [Sometimes I] wonder if [we] live in different
worlds.' The English factory's branch chairman to a conference
of lay union officials of the British rubber industry.

'The issue is ... whether any government so constituted, so
dedicated to the principles of consent and consensus within our
democracy can lead the nation.' Then Prime Minister Harold
Wilson to the mineworkers' conference, July 1975. From 'The
Economist' (12 July 1975).

THE SOURCES OF DISORDER IN THE WORKPLACE

In his well-known review of C. Wright Mills's 'The Power Elite,'
Parsons noted that Mills sees power 'exclusively as a facility for
getting what one group, the holders of power, wants by preventing
another group, the "outs," from getting what it wants' (1957, p.
139). According to Parsons this view overlooked a crucial reason
for the unequal distribution of power, namely the role of concentrated power as a resource for achieving collective goals. For this
purpose certain groups have been given 'the capacity to mobilize the
resources of society for the attainment of goals for which a general
"public" commitment has been made or may be made' (ibid., p.140).
  Among other things, this study has tried to show how the dispersion of power in the English factory had weakened the capacity of
those in positions of formal authority to provide the coordination

necessary to achieve collective - or at any rate complementary - goals. These goals, it was also shown, were not attainable through the uncoordinated actions of separate groups in the workplace. The reason that they were not attainable in this way has already been described in chapter 1. There it was pointed out, following Schelling, that individual choices, each made separately and so without taking account of the interaction between them, may combine to produce a worse result for the individuals involved than could have been obtained by coordinating the choices to take account of their interaction.

We saw in an earlier chapter that, while pay was the major pre-occupation in each factory, it was less pay levels as such than differentials that concerned the workers. (1) In other words, workers tended to define their pay objectives in terms of the earnings of other workers. For the most part their goals were limited to maintaining their relative position in the factory's earnings hierarchy. However, in the English factory this goal was constantly frustrated by the disorder in the pay system. The English pay structure was the result of hundreds of isolated bargains struck with management by different groups of workers. Consequently it reflected accidents of bargaining strength and technical change rather than 'fair' or customary pay relationships. In the face of the inability of management and their own representatives to restore equity to the pay structure, work groups in the English factory turned to self-help. This resort to fractional bargaining, however, in no way implied a repudiation of the normative consensus concerning proper pay relationships in the factory; rather it resulted from the growing discrepancy between that consensus and the actual structure of earnings. Work groups took the law into their own hands not in defiance of the consensus but because the consensus was no longer being effectively administered and enforced. There was, in other words, no normative breakdown but rather a breakdown of government in the workplace.

It should be noticed, too, that the war of all against all in the English factory stemmed from conflict and competition within the workforce. The disorder was not the result of conflict between labor and management but of the competition between different groups of workers in the workplace. In this competition, as Fox and Flanders have pointed out (1970, p.257), the 'issue is the distribution of rewards and privileges not *between* classes but *within* classes.... The post-war situation, by unleashing powerful competitive forces between groups and sections among wage and lower-salary earners, makes this fact far more palpable and insistent than it has ever seemed before. The jostling for advantage between groups is currently on an unprecedented scale.' In these circumstances, and because of the inflation resulting from them, no group of workers has a realistic option to stay out of the competition; in self-defense they are compelled to resort to the same tactics of disruption used successfully by other, more aggressive, groups. Therefore appeals to conscience are bound to fall on deaf ears. As Flanders has remarked:

> Asking the bargaining parties to take the public interest into
> account must be ineffective as long as the interpersonal forces
> of the system compel them to act differently.... However great

the parties' sense of social responsibility they cannot afford to
lose their place in the race. Their behaviour, in other words,
is not freely chosen; it is structured by the conditions in
which they operate (Flanders, 1970, p.165).

In the German factory, by contrast, the groups possessing formal
authority were able to supply the coordination, backed up by coercion when needed, which was required to maintain a structure of
earnings that was generally recognized as legitimate. The centralized and expert determination of piecework values made possible a
more coherent pay structure; there was considerably greater freedom
to correct such anomalies as did arise; and the fact that pay decisions were being made by people above the battle and beholden to
no particular groups in the workplace relieved workers of the need
to be on constant watch over their own interests.

Paradoxically, then, management and works council in the German
factory were able to maintain a pay structure that had broad legitimacy in the eyes of the workforce precisely because they were able
to withstand the pressures of the workforce - or, more exactly, the
contradictory pressures of different groups among the workforce.
According to Dahrendorf's analysis, this relative insulation from
the shop floor might have been expected to lead to alienation and
even rebellion among the workforce. On the evidence of this study,
however, it would appear that excessive openness to the shop floor
is likely to weaken the capacity of the formal institutions to integrate different sectional interests among the workforce, and the
resulting disorder is even more likely to bring those institutions
into discredit. In post-war conditions, the latter danger seems to
be the greater one.

ALTERNATIVE EXPLANATIONS OF DISORDER: A RECONSIDERATION

These findings regarding the disorder in the British workplace
enable us to specify one of the principal weaknesses of the alternative explanations examined in chapter 1. What several of these explanations (the neo-Durkheimian, collectivist, and Marxist) have in
common is that they neglect processes at the micro level, i.e., on
the shop floor. This neglect apparently reflects an unspoken assumption that the relationship between aggregate outcomes and micro-
decisions is fairly direct and unproblematic. That being assumed,
it is a straightforward matter to infer from the results of workers'
actions what their states of mind must have been. (This is a vari-
ant of the fallacy of composition.) Instead, this study has shown
that micro-level actions may interact in such a way as to produce an
outcome desired by no one.

In his (neo-Durkheimian) account, Goldthorpe infers from the disorder in British industry that there has been a breakdown of normative consensus. However, we have seen that this consensus is largely intact but is nevertheless quite powerless to influence behavior
so long as the means for its implementation are lacking. If a re-
calcitrant minority can repeatedly flout the norms with impunity,
then they will begin to lose their hold over the majority, even if
their moral basis remains unquestioned. In other words, the existence of a substantial degree of normative consensus is by itself

no guarantee of broad compliance with its terms; for that to happen
the consensus must be administered - and if necessary, imposed - by
some form of government.

A similar criticism can be directed at Beer's collectivist model
of British politics. At the risk of oversimplification, one can say
that Beer's analysis is mostly limited to the interactions of the
large collective actors on the British scene - political parties,
interest groups, trade unions, etc. Less attention is given to the
strains that may be generated within these organizations by their
participation in the new group politics, particularly in their relations with their rank-and-files. Insofar as leadership-base relations are treated at all, it is as a function of political culture.
Thus, at least in the first edition of 'British Politics,' rank-and-
file compliance is treated as relatively unproblematic because the
new group politics are congruent with values and beliefs deeply embedded in British political culture. And when he later tries to
account for the failures of the new group politics, Beer is inclined
to diagnose the problem as one of inadequate 'mobilization of consent.' Largely absent from this analysis is any sense that structural constraints in the workplace may cause workers to act in ways
that cumulatively may frustrate government policies, although that
consequence is in no way intended - and, indeed, may be deplored -
by them.

Marxist approaches to understanding industrial disorder are
especially prone to this confusion of levels of analysis. They are
bound to interpret the disorder as a sign of at least latent class
conflict. But, as this study has shown, the disorder in the British
workplace typically sets worker against worker, and the grievances
that fuel the disorder are typically very limited in scope and are
not articulated with any class-wide grievances. At the heart of the
disorder is the instability of pay and work relations between groups
of workers in individual workplaces. Indeed, by exacerbating divi-
sive jealousies between workers, the disorder may actually retard
the growth of class-consciousness. For example, the instability of
pay relations within the workplace may focus attention on local inequities and away from larger inequalities in the distribution of
earnings.

Marx was aware of the pitfalls involved in identifying the interests of the working class with those of individual workers. At the
theoretical level, this problem was resolved by postulating that the
conditions of the working class would everywhere become identical.
By obliterating all distinctions between workers and by reducing
them all to 'paid wage laborers,' capitalism would give them the
same objective interests and so would lay the basis for their cooperation in its eventual overthrow. The reality that is exhaus-
tively documented in this study is that sectional rivalries within
the British working class are intense and are the principal source
of the endemic conflict in British industry. It is in Germany, precisely because the fragmentation of labor has been held in check
there, that the unions have the capacity to act as vehicles of the
collective interests of the working class, and have made - or have
threatened to make - the more radical inroads into the capitalist
organization of the economy (for example, through the extension of
co-determination at board level). It would follow that a precon-

dition for effective collective action by British workers is the
stabilization of intra-class pay and work relations. Only with a
truce on those issues might it be possible to broaden workers'
frames of reference to encompass inter-class inequalities. If this
analysis is correct, then far from being an expression of class conflict, the disorder in the British workplace is its antithesis. (2)

Another way of describing the error shared by these approaches is
to say that they arbitrarily limit themselves to political explanatory variables. (3) Because industrial disorder has resisted repeated attempts to find political solutions, it is interpreted as a
political failure and its causes are looked for in the sphere of
politics. Or, to put the point another way, it is assumed that the
macro-level outcomes are more or less willed by the microactors. If
government policies have failed, then it must be because they have
not rallied enough support: either, the industrial disorder reflects a breakdown at the grassroots of the normative consensus
supporting the economic system; or, the stalemate of the new group
politics is attributable to the inadequate mobilization of popular
consent; or, the industrial disorder represents the opening skir-
mishes of a coming class war.

It is my view that all three approaches underestimate the extent
to which public policy may be defeated by the unintended consequences of micro-level actions whose motivations are entirely
apolitical. The endemic disorder in British industry is not the
result of a challenge to the legitimacy of the larger economic and
political system; the disorder may, of course, threaten that
system, but that is an unintended consequence of actions taken by
workers in response to entirely local concerns. The fallacy of
these approaches, then, consists in their confusion between subjective motives and objective consequences, (4) and more particularly in their tendency to infer the former from the latter.

Also, while workers' actions are influenced by macrosociological
entities - unions, employers' organizations, government - this influence is typically indirect, i.e., mediated by structures in the
workplace. That is to say, this influence makes itself felt primarily by structuring the 'logic of the situation' confronting workers
in different workplaces in each country. The remainder of this
chapter is devoted to tracing how the incidence of industrial disorder in Britain and Germany is influenced by the structure of the
larger labor relations system in each country.

NATIONAL LABOR RELATIONS SYSTEMS AND INDUSTRIAL DISORDER

In chapter 3 I described how post-war conditions had subverted the
regulatory power of industry-wide collective bargaining agreements
by vastly increasing the scope and opportunity for bargaining at the
factory level. Full order books and chronic labor shortages had
weakened employers' resistance to wage demands arising in the workplace (Clegg, 1976, p.66). However, while in Britain this development had led to the dispersal of power within the workplace as well,
and thus to the war of all against all described in these pages, in
Germany works councils and managements had by and large been able to
retain control over pay and to administer stable and orderly wage
structures.

In the final part of my study I identify some of the ways in which the principal structural components of the British and German systems of labor relations - viz. unions, employers' organizations, and the state - have contributed to the weakness or strength of the formal institutions in the workplace. Specifically, I show how the national systems of labor relations have affected the capacity of workplace institutions to stem the dispersion of power on the shop floor. Since I did not directly investigate the national systems, the following account is based for the most part on secondary sources. As such it does not represent 'findings' but rather hypotheses generated by my research.

The most ambitious attempt to relate differences in union behavior (especially strike activity) in systematic fashion to differences in collective bargaining is Clegg's 'Trade Unionism under Collective Bargaining' (1976). (5) The following discussion is largely indebted to this work, although it diverges from it on a few significant points. Most notably, I see the 'level of bargaining' (Clegg's principal explanatory variable) largely as a function of 'union structure' (i.e., 'the coverage by unions of industries and grades of employees,' ibid., p.9) as well as the cohesion of employers. Clegg, on the other hand, apparently would not agree that union structure has significantly influenced the level of bargaining in British and German industry.

Union structure

Why has no effective system of workplace 'government' developed in Britain to fill the vacuum left by the breakdown of industry-wide regulation of labor relations? In particular, why has the shop steward system been unable to assert control over the warring sectional interests in the workplace? One important reason for the weakness of labor representation inside the plant, I believe, is the structure of organized labor outside the plant.

In Britain, as is well known, unions are usually organized along general or craft lines; in Germany industrial unions predominate. (6) Although in Britain 'There have been waves of amalgamation ... which have greatly reduced the total number of unions [these] have done nothing to simplify the overall pattern. Instead they have strung together groups of members and areas of recognized bargaining rights in ever more incomprehensible confusion' (Clegg, 1976, p.32). As a result, it is not unusual in Britain for workers in the same factory - and even within the same grade - to belong to different unions. We have already seen how this can hinder cooperation between different parts of the workforce. Turner et al. (1967, p. 206) have noted that in the British automobile industry

> when workplace bargaining became the key determinant of employment terms and conditions, however, [the loose cooperation between unions with members in the industry] no longer sufficed to provide the intricate and detailed coordination now required between different unions' members and officers.... The national unions have so far been unable - indeed have made small attempt - to develop an organization to give the detailed guidance that coordination at the workplace level would require (especially since

on some of the questions involved they have been at variance with
each other).
This arrangement also commonly leads to competitive wage bargaining
between the unions in the workplace.

But the structure of British unions has had still more fateful
consequences for their capacity to exercise control over their rank
and file. The reason for this is that the members of one general
union are potential members of any other general union; if they are
dissatisfied with their union's policies, or do not feel that their
interests are being adequately represented, they can defect to another union. (7) Industrial unions, by contrast, enjoy a monopoly
over the representation of workers within a given industry.

This has meant that British unions are locked into a state of
latent competition over members. It makes no difference that this
competition only occasionally surfaces in overt hostilities; the
ever-present possibility of defections conditions the behavior of
British unions.

In these circumstances unions have been unable to stop their
members from breaking ranks and pursuing their sectional interests
through workplace bargaining. Any attempt to do so would run the
risk of driving the members - and their dues with them - into the
arms of rival unions. Thus, while 'a few unions have occasionally
disciplined stewards [for staging actions in violation of union
rules and agreed disputes procedures] ... competition between unions
for members, often with militancy as the cutting edge, has limited
the application of this sanction, despite the advice of the TUC'
(Goodman and Whittingham; 1969, pp.183-4). The same consideration
led the Donovan Commission to reject proposals requiring unions to
exercise greater discipline over their members; such a course, the
Commission said, was 'more likely to lead to internal disruption in
the unions than to a reduction in unofficial strikes' (1968, p.130).

The latent competition for members has also played a part in another structural weakness of British unions that has limited their
capacity to influence shopfloor behavior, namely the small number
of full-time trade union officials. The reason for this is that,
in comparison with German and American unions, British unions have
generally been chronically underfinanced owing to the fact that
union dues are very much lower in Britain. While the lack of appeal
of trade unionism for instrumentally oriented workers has no doubt
contributed to this situation, the 'general problem of organizational competition for members' (Latta, 1972, p.410) has been its main
cause.

For these reasons, British unions have little ability or inclina-
tion to restrain sectional demands by groups of their workers.
Indeed, because they typically have organized only a part of the
workforce of an industry or workplace, they themselves are likely
to take a sectional view of disputes that arise there. They have
no stake in the integrity of the industry's or workplace's pay
structure; they are simply concerned to ensure that their own
members' interests are protected.

In Germany, by contrast, unions are likely to oppose demands by
sections of their memberships. They are likely to do so in the
interests of their own organizational stability and survival: as
industrial unions they represent all workers within a given work-

place regardless of grade or occupation, and their unity is
threatened if individual groups of workers secure unilateral concessions from management. (8)

Just as the logic of fragmented and overlapping union membership
leads British unions to support (or at any rate not to restrain) the
sectional interests of their members in a given workplace, so the
logic of industrial unionism leads German unions to play an integrative role in the workplace. (9)   Outbreaks of inter-group rivalry
are limited by the fact that all workers are covered by the same
agreement;   and when such outbreaks occur German unions are less
ready to oppose management's attempts to bring them under control.

The same logic impels the German works council to play an integrative role within the factory. The works council is charged by
law with representing all the employees in a particular workplace
and not just certain classes of them;   and works councillors are not
elected by different constituencies but by the workforce as a whole.
Other arrangements also counteract tendencies towards fragmentation
or towards the formation of local power bases by individual councillors.   First, the actions of the works council are legally valid
only if they are collective.   In practical terms this means that a
majority of councillors is required;   the council may delegate all
of its powers (with the exception of the power to conclude 'plant
agreements') to its executive committee;   but such a delegation of
powers must be in written form and must be approved by a majority of
councillors.   Second, in the usual case candidates do not run for
seats on the council individually but as part of a slate or list of
candidates;   the candidate's position on the list crucially influences his chances of election.   Third, the works councillors' comparative security of tenure and their statutory obligations en-
courage a degree of independence from sectional demands and pressures.   Fourth, the works council's effectiveness at protecting the
interests of the workforce does not depend on its capacity or
willingness to mobilize the workforce for some form of industrial
action;   in Germany remedies are available through a variety of
other channels, e.g., the labor courts and arbitration. (10)   Apart
from making possible a measure of industrial disarmament, this
factor strengthens the council's independence vis-à-vis the workforce.   (By contrast, until recently the sole means of challenging
unfair dismissals in Britain was to turn them into industrial disputes. (11)   British unions have traditionally opposed statutory
protections for workers, as in this case, (12) and have preferred
to retain a monopoly of the available remedies.)

To recapitulate: in Germany, both inside and outside the workplace, the official institutions of labor representation enjoy a
monopoly over the representation of the workforce.   This has at
least two consequences: (i) Official leaders (i.e., union and works
council) can oppose powerful sectional interest groups without risk-
ing defections to another union or the founding of a competing,
parallel structure of labor representation within the workplace.
(The works council cannot be displaced;   its members can only be
replaced in periodic elections.)   (ii) Furthermore, unions and works
council have an actual incentive to oppose (and, if necessary, to
support management in disciplining) such groups because of the
threat they pose to the workforce's harmony and solidarity.

The result is that, in the German context, it is difficult for
sectional interests to secure a foothold. As Streeck (1981, p.157)
notes:

> One example of an interest that is unlikely to be taken up by
> either an industrial union or a works council is that of privi-
> leged sections of the workforce in the preservation of their
> status against industrial change. Another would be the interest
> of a group of workers in improving its position in the wage
> structure, or the claim of an occupational group to an exclusive
> right to do a certain kind of work. In the existing institution-
> al system such interests do not confront the employer directly
> but have first to find the internal approval of the other special
> interest groups also represented by the industrial union or the
> works council. In this way they are exposed to *a dynamic of com-
> promise and coalition building* which forces them to accommodate
> themselves with other, sometimes conflicting, interests and thus
> softens their sectional 'irresponsibility.' (13)

Employers' organizations

Clegg (1976) has persuasively argued that unions' authority over
their members may be crucially influenced by the degree of organization and the policies of employers:

> Although union constitutions and methods of administration have
> an effect on the distribution of power and the extent of faction-
> al conflict within unions ... the level of bargaining is the
> primary explanatory variable. Industry bargaining concentrates
> power in the centre, whereas bargaining power at lower levels
> disperses it.... The main influence on the level of collective
> bargaining is the structure of management and employers' associ-
> ations (ibid., p.54).

Why should the cohesion of employers have any implications for power
relations within unions? The answer, of course, has to do with the
resources that can be mobilized by either side in a collective bargaining confrontation. Outside support can greatly increase the
bargaining strength of the side receiving it. Thus, if the bargaining strength of an individual employer is enhanced by employer
solidarity, his employees in turn will become more dependent on
their union for its countervailing support. (In this way there can
result a sort of symbiosis between unions and employers' organizations.)

In chapter 6 I drew attention to the interdependence of the power
of shop stewards and management in the English factory. In particular, management's loss of control over pay had seriously undermined
the influence of shop stewards over their districts. To what extent
can the inability of the British shop steward system to integrate
the interests of workers in the workplace be explained in terms of
the weakness of British management?

One does not have to look far to find such explanations in the
literature on British labor relations. For example, Flanders (1970,
p.122) has said that 'management is apt ... merely to react to union
pressures. It concedes nothing of substance until coerced by
threats or a show of force, and then capitulates. When the lesson

is made so clear that only coercion pays off, it becomes the very
height of absurdity to ask the unions to prevent their members from
acting on it.' Turner et al. (1967, p.345) reported that union
leaders in the British automobile industry blamed its strike-prone-
ness on the 'willingness of individual firms to make concessions, in
response to unofficial pressures, which they would not make when
these were requested through "procedure" - thus themselves demon-
strating that unofficial strikes paid off.' (14) (Though it should
be added that Turner and his colleagues did not share this view.)
In a similar vein, Garbarino (1973, p.799) has suggested that the
reason for the absence of means of settling disputes by arbitration
or through the courts in Britain 'seems to be that the traditional
use of direct action in local disputes produces for most unions
better results.' At a conference on incomes policy a union spokesman pointed out that 'unions cannot say no to an outstretched hand
offering more money' (Blackaby, 1972, p.5). Clegg (1976, p.62) has
said that while Swedish unions have exercised strong control over
their members, 'the main credit for enforcing agreements belongs to
the employers. If like many British employers in the postwar
period, they were prepared to make workplace concessions which over-
rode the agreements, neither the unions nor the procedure could stop
them.'

There is some support for this line of explanation in the case of
the English factory. For example, the branch traced the deterioration of the factory's labor relations to a strike by the engineers
in 1974. On that occasion management had disregarded its own rules
and had agreed to negotiate with the engineers while they were still
out on strike. From that time on, I was told, the branch had been
unable to convince its members that management would refuse to dis-
cuss their grievances until they had resumed work. Such arguments
simply drew the scornful response: 'They talked to the engineers,
didn't they?'

However, it will be recalled that in chapter 2 we turned up no
material differences between the two factories' managements.
(Indeed, the company was chosen with a view to minimizing differences in this regard.) In that case, if management was weaker in
the English factory, this weakness cannot be explained in terms of
characteristics of the English management; but it may be explicable
in terms of the collective weakness of British employers as compared
with their German counterparts.

In Germany the power of management in the workplace is strength-
ened by the remarkable solidarity of German employers. This
solidarity is administered by a network of highly organized and
well-disciplined employers' associations; 'taken altogether, the
many associations and layers of federations and committees completely blanket employer interests' (Kerr, 1957, p.176). It is worth describing some of the obligations that firms typically incur towards
those of their number who are struck: (i) The employers' association administers a strike protection fund from which struck firms
may be compensated. (ii) A struck firm may be entitled to receive
shipments of supplies and materials from other firms; and these
other firms may be required to place transport and/or production
facilities at the disposal of the struck firm. (iii) Other firms
may not entice customers away from the struck firm; nor may they

transfer their own orders to other suppliers. (iv) Other firms may
not hire striking employees away from the struck firm. (15)   (v) The
association may require other firms to lock out their employees.   In
contrast to Britain, where the lockout is virtually unknown, German
employers have not been reluctant to use this sanction, particularly
in cases where unions have tried to 'whipsaw' them into making concessions. (16)   The German unions have challenged the legality of
the lockout in the courts (see Zachert, 1978, p.280).

German employers' associations are empowered to take measures to
bring errant members back into line.   Apart from custom and social
pressure,

> selective price cutting has been practiced against the non-
> conformist, or purchasers at the next stage in the productive
> process have been advised not to deal with him, or exhibition
> at fairs has been made difficult or impossible.... Banking
> institutions, with their control over credit availability, can
> be and have been used as enforcement agencies.... Actually this
> power is not often used for disciplinary purposes. Its adequacy
> makes its application infrequent (Kerr, 1957, p.173).

In addition, member firms who break ranks may be (and on occasion
have been) expelled.

Where both sides of industry are so highly organized it is very
difficult for a company to go it alone, as Ford Motor Company discovered.   Ford had made a practice of remaining aloof from em-
ploers' associations (as in Britain, for example).   However, in 1963
it was struck by the giant metalworkers' union (IG Metall).   Reichel
(1973, pp.257-8) describes what followed:

> The union called a lawful strike against Ford because it refused
> to enter into an enterprise-level agreement proposed by the
> union. The collective agreement covering other firms in the
> industry in the same area was still in force, and the parties
> to it were bound by its industrial peace clause. Ford then
> joined the employers' association which meant that it was auto-
> matically covered by the agreement in question and was thereby
> protected by the industrial peace clause obliging the union to
> call off the strike.

In Britain employers' associations seem pallid in comparison with
their German counterparts.   Clegg (1970, p.141) says that 'the importance attached to collective action by employers has declined
over the years.'   While 'some associations offer a financial in-
demnity to members involved in stoppages ... this practice seems to
be a relic of the nineteenth century, for it is almost unknown in
associations formed in the present century' (ibid., pp.140-1).   The
Engineering Employers' Federation told the Donovan Commission that
'the advantages' of belonging to the Federation 'are such as would
accrue from membership of any "club"' (ibid., p.143).

The lack of cohesion of British employers makes it difficult for
the individual employer to resist wage pressures.   A stoppage might
lead to the loss of important customers in addition to its direct
economic cost.   In a tight labor market the employer cannot afford
to allow his workforce's earnings to increase at a slower rate than
those in neighboring companies.   Consequently, if his hands are tied
by incomes policy, he may find it difficult to oppose unofficial,
under-the-counter increases that enables his wages to keep pace with

the wage drift elsewhere (even though he is aware of the damage that will result to his pay structure). In Germany, the employers' associations provide a vital degree of coordination of member firms' wage policies that restrains inflationary competition among employers for scarce labor. If an employer tries to 'pirate' labor by granting too many wage (or non-wage) concessions he may invite the sanctions of the employers' association (Kerr, 1957, p.173). At the same time, the individual employer is better able to withstand shop-floor pressures because he knows that a strike will not place him at a competitive disadvantage. In these ways the solidarity of German employers has contributed to orderly factory and industry wage structures. Furthermore, the employers' solidarity has had the paradoxical effect of strengthening the influence of unions and works councils over their rank-and-file; by enabling employers to resist piecemeal concessions on the shop floor it has obliged workers to look to their official representatives for the satisfaction of their demands.

The state

In both Britain and Germany the state has deeply influenced the conduct of labor relations in the post-war years; but their influence has made itself felt in quite opposite ways. In Germany, the state has established a detailed framework of laws for the regulation of labor relations but then has largely let them take their course. British governments, on the other hand, have abstained from tampering with the system itself but have attempted to control its consequences. (It is true that this contrast has become somewhat blurred over the last ten years.)

The different approaches can be illustrated by comparing the two countries' attempts to limit wage inflation. As we saw in chapter 1, since the war the policies of successive British governments have reflected a common collectivist inspiration. Both Labour and Conservative governments have tried to enlist the cooperation of organized labor and organized business in the management of the economy. This has meant that policies have generally been determined by a process of bargaining with interested producer groups; the object has been to reach a consensus which will then largely be implemented by the groups themselves. The prime example of this process is the repeated attempts to devise and operate an incomes policy. In the post-war years, as Beer (1969, p.422) has noted, 'the success of planning depended upon the restraint of inflation.' One government after another has therefore tried to negotiate with business and, in particular, with labor the terms on which they would be ready to support wage and price restraint. 'After Labour took office in 1964 ... at the heart of the Government's economic problems were relations with organized labor.... Although pursued with unbelievable patience and the utmost sensitivity to the feelings of the unions, incomes policy under Labour was significantly, but not sufficiently, more successful than it had been under the Conservatives' (ibid., pp.411-12).

Why has a viable incomes policy proved to be beyond the reach of successive British governments? The findings of my study make it

possible to suggest certain tentative answers. First, it is doubtful whether an incomes policy is workable for more than a short
period under any circumstances. Incomes policy treats symptoms
while leaving the underlying condition untouched: it does not place
an employer in a stronger bargaining relationship with a strategically placed group of workers; nor does it enable an expanding
company to attract additional workers without offering better wages;
nor, as we have seen, does it prevent the growth of distortions in a
factory's wage structure. Consequently, 'incomes policies, however
rational and enlightened they may appear when looked at at the
macro-level, necessarily become arbitrary and unacceptable when seen
at the micro-level.... Such arbitrariness is occasionally tolerated
for a few months in a fit of national fervour; but it never has and
never could last longer' (Jay, 1976, p.20).

Second, British governments have seriously overestimated the cohesion of producer groups and their capacity to lead their members.
For reasons that we looked at in the preceding two sections, British
employers and unions are singularly badly organized for imposing coherent policies on their grass roots.

Third, incomes policy may actually undermine its own foundations
by placing intolerable strains on the structures of the producer
groups; and it may also damage the labor relations system's own
native ability to restrain wage inflation and disorder. By co-
opting union leadership, British governments have helped to detach
it from its own rank-and-file. As anomalies have multiplied, unions
have been unable to take the lead in correcting them, and the initiative has therefore passed to unofficial leaders. Incomes policy
must bear a large share of the blame for having driven wage bargaining into the interstices of the official system. Moreover, in
seeking to create a climate favorable to the cooperation of unions,
governments have often acquiesced in or actually promoted inflationary wage settlements: [17] the need to protect the consensus has
engendered a marked aversion to industrial conflict [18] (far in
excess of that imputed to German governments by Dahrendorf). The
same reasons have inhibited attempts at structural reforms of
British labor relations. Finally, it is probable, too, that employers' self-reliance has been weakened by eleventh-hour inter-
ventions in the public interest that have undercut their resistance.
[19]

German governments, it is true, have attempted to influence the
growth of wages through their policy of 'concerted action.' However, this policy has been largely confined to exhorting unions to
orient their wage claims to national economic forecasts; it has
never taken the form of a rigid pay norm. [20] It is interesting
to note that the unions' restraint nevertheless appears to have contributed to the wave of 'spontaneous' strikes of September 1969.
'The strikes were an unintended consequence of the Government's
policy on incomes' (Bergmann et al., 1975; p.323; see also Witley,
1974). Bergmann and his colleagues attribute the 1974 strikes to
the same cause (ibid., p.324). It would appear that even under the
German system wage restraint may generate some of the shopfloor
pressures that we observed in Britain. Any prolonged experiment
with a rigid incomes policy might therefore be expected to weaken
German institutions and to lead to British-style disorder in German
labor relations.

CONCLUSION

If the preceding analysis is correct, wage inflation and industrial disorder are rooted in the structure of British labor relations; consequently they are not susceptible of direct political manipulation. Past remedies failed, not because they were unable to obtain popular consent, but because they were frustrated and deflected by the structural constraints identified in these pages; it follows that future remedies are unlikely to have any lasting effect if they leave the roots of the disorder intact.

THE PERFORMANCE OF THE TWO FACTORIES COMPARED

In this appendix I compare the performances of the two factories in terms of various measures of economic efficiency.

LABOR PRODUCTIVITY

The German factory was performing at a substantially higher level of labor productivity than the English factory. According to my estimate, the output of radial passenger tires per German production worker was 63 per cent higher than that of the English production worker. (1)

In view of the methodological pitfalls that bedevil comparisons of productivity, (2) it is worth spelling out how this estimate was arrived at. 'Labor productivity' refers, of course, to measures of the output of a given product obtained for each unit of labor input. Before I could compare the productivity of the two factories, then, I had to find standardized measures of their output and of the labor employed to produce that output.

The measurement of output

Finding a common basis on which to compare the output of the two factories was complicated by differences in the range and mix of tires that they manufactured. Each factory produced passenger, truck and rear tractor-tires; however, the English factory manufactured crossply and fabric radial in addition to steel radial models, as well as a variety of special purpose tires. In order to simplify the comparison I decided to look at only radial tire production.

This step did not entirely eliminate differences in product mix. Radial passenger tires vary in size and construction and so a crude comparison of numbers of tires produced per head might have been misleading. Fortunately the company recorded output in terms of weight as well as numbers. Since tire weight is related to tire size and - to a lesser extent - complexity, it was possible to correct the numbers of radial passenger tires produced to allow for

these differences. In practice this meant that two productivity
differentials were computed - one in terms of units and the other
in terms of weight - and the average of the two was taken. (The
resulting adjustment was a minor one; the average German radial
passenger tire was less than 10 per cent heavier than the average
English one.)

The data on which the productivity comparisons were based related
to the same nine-month period for each factory. They were taken
from the factories' monthly production reports which are prepared on
a uniform basis throughout the company.

The measurement of labor input

The measure used for labor input was the average number of production workers engaged in radial passenger tire production over the
nine-month period.

The main difficulties encountered in calculating these values
arose from the need to apportion the workforces between radial
passenger and other types of tire production. In some cases I had
insufficient information with which to make a determination and so
an entire operation or set of operations had to be excluded from the
comparison. For this reason and (more importantly) because of the
initial decision to limit the comparison to radial passenger tire
production, I was left with roughly one quarter of the English production workforce and one half of the German.

Inconsistent definitions of production and other labor would
naturally distort a comparison of output per production worker.
There was, in fact, a tendency for production workers in the German
factory to assume additional responsibilities, e.g., some supervisory tasks. As a consequence, the productivity differential may
be slightly understated.

The estimates of labor input were not weighed by different
classes of employees (for instance by nationality, age, or skill).
However, the extent of patterned differences of this sort was described in chapter 2; and the reader is left to form his own judg-
ment on the likely effects of such differences.

CAUSES OF THE PRODUCTIVITY DIFFERENTIAL

In chapter 4 I argue that the labor productivity differential between the two factories is in large part accounted for by the endemic fractional bargaining in the English factory. Obviously a
range of other factors can affect levels of labor productivity; the
possible relevance of a number of such factors to the present case
is examined in the following sections.

Factory size

As noted in chapter 2, the English factory is considerably larger
than the German one. The question therefore arises: did the
English factory's size enable it to take advantage of opportunities
for economies of scale not available to the German factory?

What exactly might these opportunities consist in? It will be recalled that our comparison was confined to production employees. The productivity of direct workers is not affected by size per se, but by the higher rates of output and longer production runs that normally accompany it. Productivity is increased by higher rates of output because of the greater scope that they provide for 'reducing the setting-up time for machinery and for maintaining an even flow of work' (Pratten, 1976, p.29). In other words, higher output is possible because of the increased ratio of productive time to non-productive (i.e., changeover or set-up) time. However, while size and rate of output are usually associated, this is not necessarily always the case. As Pratten notes, 'firms with large total output tend to be able to organize high rates of output or long production runs of individual products, but smaller firms may achieve this result by specialization' (ibid., p.28).

Thus it would be a mistake to assume a priori that the English factory was the beneficiary of greater economies of scale. In fact, as we have seen, it produced a very much more diversified range of tires than the German factory. Was the range so wide as to cancel out the opportunities for longer production runs presented by its greater size?

An exact answer to this question would be outside the scope and the means of this study. However, a rough indication was obtained by comparing the ratio of tire codes to builders in each tire room. Since each tire code denotes a unique model of tire, the greater their number the more frequently changeovers are likely to be required. On this basis it would appear that changeovers must have been marginally more frequent in Germany. However, the actual disparity was too small to be a significant source of variation in productivity.

Factory and plant

The English factory was considerably older than the German one. By itself the age of the factories probably made very little difference for, as Pratten (ibid., p.42) found, 'generally ... firms reckoned differences in the vintages of factories were not a cause of significant differences in labor productivity because new machinery could be installed at existing factories.'

As explained in chapter 2, where the age-difference did show was in the layout of the production process. There can be no doubt that the English factory's layout led to the employment of relatively more labor in materials handling. (3) In addition, it imposed other, intangible costs on the English factory's operations by hindering the coordination of production and by impeding communication between departments.

As reported in chapter 2, the two factories employed virtually identical machinery and production techniques.

Capacity utilization

The German factory was operating at well below its physical capacity. As we saw, three years before the fieldwork half of its workers
had been dismissed; and although the workforce was being steadily
rebuilt it was still far short of its physical limit. The effects
of this were evident less in the underutilization of equipment
(though in several departments equipment was worked only two out of
three shifts) than in the amount of unused floor space. The floor
area per production worker in the German factory was over twice that
in the English factory. For reasons that are considered in chapter
2, it appears probable that this contributed to the labor productivity differential. (4)

Management

Chapter 2 also presents reasons for concluding that the factories'
managements were very similar. It would follow that they cannot be
the source of the productivity differential.

OTHER MEASURES OF PERFORMANCE

The labor productivity differential reported in the preceding pages
does not reflect other important aspects of the performance of the
two factories. Since output is compared only in terms of the labor
needed to produce it, the other resources that are employed are ignored. The data displayed in Table A.1 provide an additional index
of the relative efficiency of the factories.

TABLE A.1

	Germany (=100)	England
Inventory levels *		
Raw materials	100	214
Stores **	100	8
Work-in-process - tires	100	189
Work-in-process - total	100	143
Waste losses ***	100	206

*   Source: Monthly Factory Statistics. Original figures were
       expressed as 'days in stores.'
**   Plainly this discrepancy is so large that it must be attributa-
       ble to different accounting methods or exceptional circum-
       stances.
***   Source: Monthly Factory Statistics.

The table shows that the German factory was able to operate with a significantly lower ratio of inventories; it also shows that the losses due to wastage of materials in the manufacturing process in the German factory were running at half the rate in the English factory.

Stability of production

Melman (1958, p.165) has noted that stability of production tends to be positively associated with higher average levels of productivity. The reason for this is that 'the reduction of variability within the system can put the system into better balance. Fewer delays and greater smoothness of internal production rates yields a higher productivity level for the system as a whole.'

For the month of September 1977 I obtained the daily production reports for each passenger tire room. Following Melman (ibid., p. 166), I computed the coefficient of variation for daily production in the course of the month (i.e., the standard deviation expressed as a percentage of the mean daily production). This coefficient measures the variability of production from day to day. The coefficients for the tire rooms were:

Germany	11.3 per cent
England	22.0 per cent

It should be noted that the lower German figure was achieved in spite of the smaller output of the German tire room and much greater fluctuations in manning levels.

Quality of product

Since each factory was producing the same (or, at least, a broadly overlapping) range of tires, to the same company-wide specifications, and for sale world-wide under the same brand name, one might have expected only slight variations in quality. In fact there was evidence that market constraints compelled the German factory to meet more stringent quality standards:

(i) A larger proportion of the German factory's sales were to the original equipment (as distinguished from the replacement) market. (This may be explained by the German factory's relative newness and lack of an established market position.) The original equipment market for tires is dominated by the large automobile manufacturers whose monopsonistic market strength enables them to insist on rigorous quality standards.

(ii) The weakness of the pound sterling on the international exchange markets had given the English factory a cost advantage. This appeared to have led to volume being given a high priority; in 1976 a manager had told the factory works council: 'We have an advantage cost-wise on the European market. It is just a question of getting the tires out.' (5)

(iii) It was my impression that the German domestic market is more quality-conscious than the British.

In addition to this circumstantial evidence, there were the company's own evaluations of product quality. The German factory consistently out-performed the English one by a wide margin on the company's inter-plant quality control ratings. (6) In the German factory the chairman of the works council had proposed to management (apparently not in a facetious spirit) that 'Made in Germany' be embossed in white on all tires produced there!

Other indicators of performance

Of course, there was a variety of data to which I did not have access; and in other cases only impressionistic evidence was available. By the time of my second visit to the English factory signs were already in evidence on the shop floor that the economic crisis had caught up with it. Through the production workers' grapevine I learnt that the warehouse was full; a notice posted in the factory informed employees that customers had cancelled orders for particular tire sizes and models because of delivery and quality problems; and so on. The factory's deteriorating economic position appeared to have engendered a pervasive sense of defeatism among the workforce; one branch officer said that 'the best thing would be to close down the plant and start all over again.' In spite of the German factory's brush with closure, or perhaps because it had once come back from the brink, there was widespread confidence that the factory could sustain the level of productivity and quality necessary to ride out the storm.

CONCLUSION

While any quantitative estimate is bound to be approximate, it is safe to conclude that labor productivity was substantially higher in the German factory. On a wide variety of other indicators, as well, the German factory's performance was clearly superior.

NOTES

CHAPTER 1   DISORDER IN BRITISH INDUSTRY

1   For example, data reported by Roberti (1978) for eighteen advanced industrial countries indicate that income is more equally
distributed only in Norway and New Zealand. Sawyer (1976) has
estimated the share of after-tax income going to the richest 10
per cent of households to be 23.5 per cent in the UK, and 30.3
per cent in Germany. For a review of findings concerning rates
of social mobility, see Parkin (1972, ch.4); these show that,
in comparison with other Western countries, the UK shows the
greatest degree of 'openness' in its opportunity structure.

2   Goldthorpe is of course aware of Runciman's findings, but he
argues that 'while restricted reference groups may inhibit
feelings of grievance over inequalities, this is not to say that
they actually motivate individuals to hold back from attempting
to improve their position' (1974a, p.224). It is difficult to
follow Goldthorpe's argument at this point. If the extreme inequality in Britain is somehow masked from British workers, or
has little subjective salience for them, then it cannot weaken
their moral integration into British economic life.

3   They also cite a survey by Behrend et al. (1967, ch.6) which
found that the specific occupational group most frequently
mentioned in reply to the question 'who do you think most deserve an early pay increase' was doctors (p.44).

4   Among other findings of this study two are especially noteworthy. 92 per cent of the workers (at Pilkingtons glass works)
said they felt no hostility to the company chairman, Lord
Pilkington, and 81 per cent said they would rather be at work
than at home even if it made no financial difference to them
(p.87).

5   Goldthorpe does not specify the level of consensus that would
suffice. As with many other consensus theorists he asserts
'merely that some "minimum" level of consensus about a certain
"critical" value is necessary to social cohesion. As this level
is never precisely specified, we cannot very easily come to
grips with the argument' (Mann, 1970, p.432).

6   See for example Lindblom's (1959) argument that a high degree of

coordination can result from a succession of fragmented mutual adjustments.

7 Noteworthy were the 'spontaneous' strike waves of September 1969 and of 1973. Partial vindication of Dahrendorf's thesis might b be found in the tendency, up to 1968 at least, for wildcat strikes to increase as a proportion of all strikes (though the share and the absolute number were still far short of the British figure). In the 1975 works council elections, communist and extreme left candidates obtained only a handful of seats. (On strikes see Bergmann et al., 1975, pp.399-404; on works council elections, Schneider, 1975.)

8 R.W.Apple, 'New York Times,' 20 July 1977. Interview with David Basnett, head of the General and Municipal Workers' Union.

9 Fosh and Jackson (1974). For the runner-up in this category see Bernard Nossiter's remarks shortly before the 'winter of discontent' that brought down the Callaghan Government: 'Two-thirds of the country now backs Callaghan's call for a 5 per cent limit on pay gains. Even more startling, the percentage of union members favoring guidelines, 69 per cent, was bigger than that for the country as a whole. This is the statistical underpinning to a spreading phenomenon here, rank-and-file workers repudiating shop stewards who seek to breach the pay limit' ('Boston Globe,' 28 October 1978, By-line London).

10 Although Panitch talks of a 'working class united against the operation' of the Industrial Relations Act (1976, p.249), Gallup data show the labor movement split down the middle on the subject. Two surveys conducted in August 1972, i.e., in the month the Act was abandoned, showed the following breakdowns of views among trade union members:

	August 17-21 %	August 24-28 %
Industrial Relations Act		
Approve	40	40
Disapprove	43	49
Don't know	17	11
Trade Unions and I.R. Act		
Reasonable	34	39
Unreasonable	53	50
Don't know	13	12
Should register		46
Should not		36
Don't know		18

11 Some evidence has already been presented supra. In addition, some of the findings of a government-sponsored survey of workplace labor relations may be noted. 72 per cent of the workers surveyed thought working through agreed grievance procedure brought more satisfactory results than industrial action; 69 per cent thought they got a fair wage (the biggest grumbles came from the professional and lower technical grades); 93 per cent of the shop stewards thought management was reasonably fair in disciplinary cases; etc. (Parker, 1973).

CHAPTER 2 RESEARCH SITE AND DESIGN

1 'Sectoral distribution of output and factor inputs as well as size and structure of companies and plants' (Panic, 1976).
2 The English factory also produced some low volume tires, e.g., aero and racing.
3 In Britain the number of working days lost per employee through strikes increases with size of plant. For other correlates of size see, e.g., Pratten (1976, p.55) and Ingham (1970, p.16).
4 For these points see Pratten (1976, pp.44-5).
5 For the view that technology significantly structures workplace behavior see especially Woodward (1958) and Sayles (1958).
6 Kuhn (1961, pp.148-9). British data tend to support Kuhn's hypothesis. Between 1966 and 1973 the British rubber industry was the ninth most 'stoppage-affected' of the approximately 150 industries distinguished in the official strike statistics (based on days lost per employee). Since 95 per cent of British strikes are unofficial these figures may suggest the relative incidence (if not the absolute level) of fractional bargaining. See the Department of Employment 'Gazette' for February 1976.
7 The summary nature of this account exposes it to Goldthorpe et al.'s (1968, p.182) strictures on the neglect of the 'wants and expectations which men *bring to* their work' and the way these shape their work behavior. However, a factory is far from being a social vacuum in which workers' dispositions and values can find frictionless expression. Goldthorpe's insistence on the priority of 'the point of view of the actors involved' (ibid., p.183) risks diverting attention from the factory's social structure and the patterns of behavior generated by it. For a useful corrective to this view see Popper, 1971, ch.14.
8 Fully half of the English production workers had been with the factory for eleven years or longer, i.e., for longer than the German factory had been in existence. In England 56 per cent of the production workers were over 40; in Germany 38 per cent of the hourly employees were over 40.
9 In the third quarter of 1977 the rates in the UK and Germany stood at 8.1 per cent and 3.6 per cent respectively (OECD, 'Economic Outlook,' No.22, December 1977, p.28).
10 The remaining third had less than six months' service with the company and so did not have this protection.
11 Guest workers (Gastarbeiter) amount to close to 10 per cent of the German labor force. The most exhaustive survey is Mehrländer (1974). Her team interviewed 1,678 guest workers in 1971 (i.e., before the government-ordered recruiting stop in 1973); the sample was matched with the population of guest workers with respect to country of origin and sex. The following profile emerges: the guest worker's orientation to his work is primarily instrumental; thus he works long hours and values overtime, piece work and shiftwork for the extra earnings that they bring. Although he may have been employed in Germany for a number of years (41 per cent of the males had been five years or longer) his ties to his native country remain strong (he remits part of his wages; in half the cases his children have stayed behind; he is probably saving in order to purchase

property there). He is satisfied with his current work and says he has not been discriminated against. However, large minorities report that the situation of foreign workers in their workplace is less favorable than that of German workers (38 per cent) and that their earnings are inferior to those of Germans in equivalent jobs (23 per cent). He has not been tied to a particular employer (57 per cent have changed jobs at least once). He is not a union member (31 per cent are, which is lower than for German workers) and is largely indifferent to the activities of the union.

12 In British industry particularly large concentrations of immigrant workers are to be found doing foundry work.

13 For a case where 'the natural cohesion of groups of Punjabi workers' in combination with inter-union competition for membership appears to have contributed to a series of disputes: see Commission on Industrial Relations (1971). Perhaps the most remarkable feature of the famous Grunwick case was the way in which the overwhelmingly Asian workforce defied mass pickets to report to work. See Rogaly (1977).

14 Absenteeism rates in Britain compare favorably with those in other European countries (cf. McBeath, 1973, p.24; Pratten, 1977, p.116; but see also Pratten, 1976, pp.56-7). In the English factory a sick pay scheme had been agreed in principle but had not yet been implemented. The introduction of such schemes in Britain has been accompanied by increases of between 2 and 4 per cent in absences from sickness (see 'The Economist,' 3 June 1978, p.125).

15 See also Collins et al., 1946, and Touraine and Ragazzi, 1961.

16 In order to protect the identity of the company no citation is given.

17 Cf. Fores et al. (1978, p.58).

18 All told I spent six weeks in the German factory and nine in the English one (the latter in two separate visits straddling the German visit).

19 In Germany each shift included an unpaid ½-hour meal break. The balance was made up by having each shift work on every third Saturday. I ignore certain other trivial variations.

20 'The Economist,' 10 February 1979, p.119.

21 'The Economist,' 15 April 1978, pp.86-7.

22 'The Economist,' 3 March 1979, pp.83-4.

23 'Manchester Guardian Weekly,' 29 April 1979, p.6.

24 'The Economist,' 3 March 1979, p.84.

25 'Guardian,' 13 March 1979, p.23.

26 'The Economist,' 10 February 1979, p.119.

27 Among the exceptions to which attention has been drawn are factory size, factory utilization, and geographical setting.

CHAPTER 3 FORMAL STRUCTURES OF WORKPLACE LABOR REPRESENTATION

1 Royal Commission on Trade Unions and Employers' Associations 1965-1968, under the chairmanship of Lord Donovan. It was the fifth Royal Commission into British labor relations in the last hundred years and the first since 1903. A Labour government,

    prodded by the Conservatives, set it up. References are to its Report, Cmnd. 3623, London, HMSO, 1968. Hereinafter the Donovan Report.

2 Cf. the remarks of George Woodcock, then General Secretary, to the Trades Union Congress in 1965: 'I would tell you flatly to your faces, you will go through the motions as unions and you will boast yourselves as unions, and already many of your members are getting three times as much as you have negotiated for them.... The trade union movement is being transformed, if not eroded, because of your lack of control already.'

3 And of some of its members. See in particular the eloquent minority report by Shonfield (Donovan, 1968, p.288).

4 See chapter 1 of the report. Donovan identified three characteristics of workplace bargaining in the UK; its autonomy, its informality, and its fragmentation (p.18). On the other hand, Donovan's remedy was far from adequate, as this study will show.

5 'Shop steward' is the generic title for any 'lay workplace representative who acts as a spokesman for his fellow workers in their day-to-day dealings with management' (Flanders, 1968, p. 52). 'Of course, in a sense there always had been a spokesman of the unions inside an establishment, once organization had started, but these were not official representatives and had no place in the constitutions of the unions' (B.C. Roberts quoted by Sturmthal, 1964, p.183).

6 A recent survey of 241 establishments found that in only 17 per cent was 'the most important level of bargaining' the national (i.e., industry-wide) one. In 75 per cent plant or company bargaining was the most important (Daniel, 1976, p.28).

7 Negotiations with one joint body of workers are more usual in British manufacturing industry (67 per cent of establishments surveyed). A substantial minority of labor representatives engaged in separate negotiations would have preferred one joint body (ibid., pp.79,81).

8 'Above all, in multi-union factories and companies the unions must be prepared to cooperate and to sign a common agreement' (Donovan, p.42).

9 According to the survey by Daniel (1976, p.76) 'plant negotiations on the union side were very frequently an amateur affair. Union negotiators were themselves predominantly lay officers [in 90 per cent of the cases]. In only about half of the cases was a full-time officer of the union, at any level, spontaneously cited as having been involved in preparing the claim....'

10 Goldthorpe et al. (1968, pp.98-9) report similar attendance figures; see also other findings concerning branch attendance summarized there.

11 'Such rules will make it reasonable to expect stewards (and their members) to act constitutionally ...' (Donovan, p.187).

12 'In many rule books shop stewards ... are mentioned only because the union relies upon them to collect subscriptions' (p.186).

13 Based on the figures for 1964-66, Donovan (p.97) reported that some 95 per cent of stoppages were due to unofficial strikes. These figures omit very small stoppages which are invariably unofficial.

14 See Commission on Industrial Relations, Report No.17, 'Facilities Afforded to Shop Stewards,' HMSO, 1971.

15 Stewards appointed deputies to cover other shifts (shift repre-
    sentatives) and in certain cases also to represent separate de-
    partments within their constituencies.
16 Representatives of the engineering and staff employees each met
    separately with management in their own works councils. So far
    as I could tell, only some of the specialist subcommittees
    (e.g., pensions) involved more than one group of workers.
17 The fate of the once common 'joint consultative committee' in
    British industry (of which this council, dating from pre-war
    years, is an example) is revealing. Its decline coincided with
    the increase in the influence and the number of shop stewards.
    According to McCarthy (1966, pp.33-6), 'few consequences of
    workplace bargaining have been so well investigated as its
    effect on joint consultative committees. Either they must
    change their character and become essentially negotiating com-
    mittees indistinguishable from ... shop-floor bargaining, or
    they are boycotted by shop stewards and, as the influence of
    the latter grows, fall into disuse.' (See also Clegg, 1970,
    pp.185-93.)
18 The best accounts are Sturmthal (1964) and Spiro (1958). For a
    report on works councillors' opinions on how it has worked in
    practice see Blume (1956).
19 By the Works Constitution Act (Betriebsverfassungsgesetz) of
    1972 which replaced (without substantially modifying) the Act
    of 1952.
20 E.g., Spiro's view (1962, p.578) which has worn thin over the
    years: 'In Britain people generally know how to conduct negoti-
    ations, say, in collective bargaining or at a meeting of the
    parent teacher association. This is less often the case in
    Germany, and hence the yearning to have procedural rules for
    such and any occasion laid down once for all in explicit legis-
    lation.'
21 For this reason the American social scientist, sensitized to the
    need to look beneath the surface for the 'informal' plant organ-
    ization, is likely to experience a sense of culture shock on
    studying German industry. One's first reaction is to suspect
    that cultural barriers are obscuring the informal processes from
    view; with enough persistence one expects in due course to
    stumble into a discrete tête-à-tête where the 'real' government
    of the factory is being conducted. In fact the formal organiza-
    tion appears largely to correspond with the reality. It may be
    noted that Spiro himself came to a similar conclusion (1958:68):
        Most of the participants in codetermination, from the ordi-
        nary worker on up to the Generaldirektor, are thoroughly
        familiar with the details of the various laws. In ordinary
        conversations about their activities they frequently quote
        chapter and verse, articles and paragraphs, critical com-
        mentaries and critiques of critical commentaries. In fact,
        it often takes considerable conversational pushing before one
        can extract a concrete statement about what actually goes on
        at board meetings, for instance, instead of a legalistic
        explanation of what Professor Paragraphenreiter says ought
        to be going on. In some cases the two are almost identical.
        At most works council meetings, several copies of the Consti-

tution of the Enterprise [i.e., Works Constitution Act] and
jurists' commentaries on it can be seen, lying on the table.
They get much use. One can no more understand the practice
of co-determination without having some knowledge of the
relevant laws than one could understand the practices of the
Pilgrim fathers without having some knowledge of the Bible.

22 The law provides for joint elections if both groups of employees
in a preliminary ballot vote to hold them. In this case no
preliminary ballot had been held; the issue had apparently not
been considered important enough to warrant it. In this connection compare Sturmthal's observation: 'The distinction between white-collar employees and manual workers in Germany ...
is well known as a main fact of German social life. It is
consecrated by law, administrative practice, and the mores of
the country' (1964, p.66).

23 Actually the process of nomination can be quite complicated and
is taken up later in this chapter.

24 However, these prerogatives are subject to the overriding
proviso that the operational needs of the plant be taken into
account. Thus on one occasion the personnel manager requested
that a works councillor withdraw from a duly called meeting of
the council and return to his department which was badly hit by
absenteeism. The request was complied with without hesitation.

25 'Once in arbitration, nearly all cases are disposed of without
dissent' (Kerr, 1957, p.195).

26 In the German chemical industry (under which the rubber industry
in the region was subsumed for collective bargaining purposes)
the collective agreement is in three parts and covers inter alia
the following matters. First, the master agreement (Mantel-
tarifvertrag) sets out norms respecting hours of work, overtime
premia, allowances for various conditions, the vacation entitle-
ments, supplementary rules governing hiring and dismissal, safeguards for employees against the consequences of rationalization
of work methods, etc. Second, the framework wage agreement
(Lohnrahmenvertrag) fixes the rules concerning job classification and the operation of incentive systems. Third, the wage
agreement (Lohntarifvertrag) sets hourly wage rates for all job
classifications. The master agreement is negotiated for the
entire chemical industry; the wage agreements are negotiated
separately for the industry on a state-by-state (Länder) basis.
The first two agreements have lives of three years; the last a
life of only one year. Separate pay agreements are negotiated
for wage and salary earners.

27 Bergmann et al. (1975, p.181) estimate that in 1970 earnings in
the chemical industry averaged 20 per cent above the rates fixed
in collective bargaining between the union and employers' association; they estimate the difference in the metalworking
industry at 24 per cent. In large firms the gap may, of course,
be much larger. See Ross's discussion of wage drift (1962, pp.
341-4).

28 See Bergmann et al., 1975, p.359, Table 20.

29 Part of the blame for this loss of influence lies with the union
movement itself. Historically it has shown an ambivalent attitude towards the extension of industrial democracy based on the

workplace. Its attention has, instead, been concentrated on winning the 'commanding heights' of the economy (soziale Gesamtstruktur). See Leminsky, 1975, p.586.

30 Where the election is contested by more than one list of candidates, 'each list supplies members for the council in the order in which the candidates are listed. This means in effect that lone wolves have little chance of getting elected, because they will not be placed at the top of the list by the dominant groups in the plant which make the nominations' (Spiro, 1958, p.90).

31 Many of the specific measures are aimed at implementing a policy of decentralized collective bargaining (betriebsnahe Tarif-politik). For discussions see Ross, 1962, pp.348ff; Bergmann et al., 1975, pp.169ff; and Sturmthal, 1964, p.76. However, although this policy is already of long standing, Ross's finding in 1962 is still valid today: 'It does not appear that the German unions have made a decisive breakthrough up to the present' (p.350).

32 See Gester, 1972, p.19.

33 For a fuller discussion see Bergmann et al., 1975, pp.176-8.

34 Only c. 3 per cent of the candidates elected in the 1975 works council elections were foreigners. Until 1972 guest workers had not been eligible to become councillors though they had been entitled to vote in the elections. Women also tend to be under-represented on works councils and this factory was no exception (though the workforce was preponderantly male). See Schneider, 1975, and Blume, 1956.

35 Compare Spiro (1958, p.115): 'Ideological and legalistic argumentation ... are more than mere façade or rationalization of special interests, even though they can be and have been used as such. They are woven into ways of thought and action.'

36 This voter turn-out is low by comparison with the national average in 1975 of about 80 per cent (Schneider, 1975). Interestingly the turn-out was higher (80 per cent) in the election of the worker director to the company's supervisory board.

37 Compare Spiro again (1962, p.578): Germans 'are reluctant to have relations with others that are not part and parcel of the status their vocational or political standing gives them.'

CHAPTER 4   DISORDER IN THE WORKPLACE

1 On this point my findings contradict Kuhn's. In the English factory work groups tended to be shifting coalitions; however, they were invariably defined by their place in the production process. For a fuller explanation see chapter 6.

2 One theme of Flanders' study of the Fawley productivity agreements is how management 'overlooked, until it was forced to take notice of it, the informal structure of organization which is intermediary between the unions and the men as individuals - the work group based on similarity of occupation, function and status' (1964, p.139).

3 Higher levels of capital investment have reinforced the power of work groups by raising the economic cost of any disruption. (See for example Clegg, 1970, p.39.)

4   The distinction between official and unofficial actions had
    become increasingly irrelevant to the realities of the work-
    place. Thus two ex-officers of the staff union were unable to
    agree on whether a 5-day strike by their members in the pre-
    ceding year had been official. Clearly the point held only
    academic interest.
5   Such tactics were common in British industry by the mid to late
    1960s. Compare Goldthorpe's comments on the disputes that broke
    out at Vauxhall following his study there:
    The patterns that disputes have followed at Vauxhall and the
    tactics used on the side of labour have been distinctive....
    Disputes, if protracted, have chiefly been waged through
    banning overtime and working to rule. Occasional attempts
    to put pressure on management by organized 'early leaving'
    have petered out unsuccessfully; and despite calls from
    militants, there has been conspicuously little enthusiasm
    for the strike weapon (Goldthorpe et al., 1968, p.196).
6   Instead they walked over to the engineers' compound and person-
    ally entered the job in the book. Presumably the use of the
    telephone had not been the subject of an explicit agreement
    with management.
7   Dispute No.27 in Table 4.1.
8   At Jay's Lupton (1963, p.168) found that 'because of the way in
    which "booking-in" was manipulated the records kept by manage-
    ment of worker performance did not represent the way in which
    time was actually spent.'
9   Calculated from each tire room's production records.
10 For a discussion of some of the difficulties see Turner et al.,
    1967, pp.45-50.
11 Cf. the opinion of the Donovan Commission (1968, p.111) that 'it
    would be seriously misleading to base one's assessment of the
    economic significance of [wildcat] stoppages merely on the tally
    of working days lost on their account.'
12 In the British automobile industry, 'it is *changes* which produce
    grounds for argument and negotiation, rather than the normal
    pace of trackwork itself.... These things are often again re-
    garded as a unilateral change in the terms of the "effort bar-
    gain"' (Turner et al., 1967, pp.169-70).
13 Pratten's (1976, p.55) sample included 35 firms operating in
    both Germany and the UK. Of these he found that 12
    specifically referred to the greater ease of introducing
    changes in Germany. Within these companies it was relatively
    'difficult' to introduce changes in equipment in the UK, and
    negotiations to obtain changes led to delays. This is im-
    portant because, for many firms, increasing productivity is a
    continuous process of making small improvements by reorgan-
    ization of production lines and adding often small items of
    equipment. In the UK, employees at many factories insisted
    on negotiating changes in pay when new machinery was intro-
    duced, and it was claimed that this was not the case in
    Germany.
14 The Devlin Committee on dock work asked 'If the employers are at
    last prepared to concede [decasualization] why should the men
    expect to be paid for accepting it?' (quoted by Jensen, 1971,

p.30). According to Hawkins (1976, p.193) a lesson of the past
years is that if management wants to introduce job enrichment
schemes it will have to pay for them. See also Kilpatrick and
Lawson, 1980, p.93.
15 Calculated from tire room production reports. Both weeks were
chosen at random.
16 Source: my notes of the meeting.
17 Compare Hunter et al.'s (1970), p.171) comment on the effects of
the seniority rule in the British iron and steel industry: 'the
mobility of the production labour force in steel is seriously
impeded by the seniority principle, and ... this can have important consequences for the success of schemes involving rede-
ployment within or between plants.'
18 Compare the statement of Moss Evans of the T&GWU: 'If I went to
a meeting of workers who were out on strike for an increase in
shift differential and suggested that workers' control was the
solution to their problem, they would throw me in the canal'
(quoted in Kilpatrick and Lawson, 1980, p.99).
19 The Department of Employment's statistics count only those
stoppages that have come to the attention of its local office
managers by way of newspaper reports or contacts with companies.
Companies do not file statutory returns. For a fuller discussion, see Turner et al., 1967, pp.52-3.
20 This is also Donovan's view. See 1968, pp.19-20.
21 Report in the London 'Sunday Times' (12 November 1978). Based
on a survey of 970 manufacturing establishments employing 50 or
more workers. The survey was conducted by Industrial Facts and
Forecasting Ltd for the Social Sciences Research Council industrial relations research unit at Warwick University.
22 Daniel's findings were further broken down. The highlights are
presented in the table below (Daniel, 1976, pp.9-11):

Experience of industrial conflict in prior 12 months
(percentages)

	All es- tablish- ments	Mass pro- duction	Over 500 employees	No. of unions: three or more
Threat	50	63	57	59
Some sanction	40	53	47	48
Strike	24	38	29	31

CHAPTER 5   THE PROCESS OF WAGE DETERMINATION IN THE TWO FACTORIES

1 According to the records of the British Department of Employment, between 1966 and 1974 84 per cent of all working days lost
in Britain were caused by disputes over pay (D. of E. 'Gazette,'
February 1976). Moreover on closer inspection many grievances
nominally over other matters are revealed as 'part of the pre-
paratory ritual of workplace bargaining' (Turner et al., 1967,
p.169). Cf. Goldthorpe et al. (1968, p.195): 'There seems
little doubt that the Vauxhall disputes have been decisively
centred on pay. Whenever other issues have been raised -

working conditions, work rules, job transfers, shiftwork, etc. - these have been more or less quickly revealed as primarily bargaining counters in a struggle over wage levels.'

2   Approximately 80 per cent in the German factory and a similar proportion in the English factory.

3   In Germany wage rates for the industry (Tariflohn) were negotiated annually by the regional employers' association and the union. Actual rates in the German factory were invariably higher (for pieceworkers at least 25 per cent higher), but they were nevertheless firmly anchored in the negotiated rate structure. In England across-the-board increases were negotiated annually by factory management and a committee of shop stewards (and ratified by the production workers in a secret ballot). In practice the amounts of the increases had been fixed by successive government pay policies which left little to be negotiated over; these policies had also precluded any restructuring of the factory's pay system (with consequences that are explored later in this chapter).

4   In 41 out of 46 establishments surveyed by Blume (1956, p.113) council chairmen reported that they had participated in the fixing of wages as opposed to simply responding to claims or complaints from individual employees. From the comments cited by Blume, it is apparent that many of the chairmen had training in work study.

5   In connection with a proposed overhaul of the English tire room's piecerate structure management had paid for two builders to attend an outside work study appreciation course. In one company studied by the Prices and Incomes Board 'management's original intention ... was that piecework prices would be determined solely by the time study.... In subsequent years, however, this system has become so distorted by both shopfloor bargaining pressures and formal negotiations that it functions very differently from the way that was originally intended' (NBPI, 1968 (Supplement), pp.51,53).

6   This resembles the situation in the British engineering (metalworking) industry where a 'mutuality' clause in the industry agreement stipulates that job values 'shall be fixed by mutual arrangement between the employer and the workman or workmen who perform the work.' According to Clegg, this clause was imposed by the employers on the unions in 1898 and its original intention was to exclude the union until direct bargaining had broken down (1970, p.268).

7   In one British factory studied by the Prices and Incomes Board a good shop steward was defined as one who spent 'at least 50 per cent of his time in the rate-fixing office, arguing' (NBPI, 1968, p.19).

8   Especially in Britain according to a study of incentive payment systems in OECD countries; 'In the British context, whatever scheme of payment by results is adopted ... it will start to deteriorate, to a greater or lesser extent, from the moment it is implemented' (OECD, 1970, p.47).

9   In his survey, Daniel (1976, p.31) found differentials between groups to be the 'most difficult problem' over pay. Cf. also the finding of a research paper for the Donovan Commission: the

'most common argument used by stewards to justify grievances and claims was appeal to some kind of comparison with another individual or group in similar circumstances or employed on similar work' (McCarthy, 1966, p.17).

10 One factor contributing towards wage drift is the assumption 'that new piece rates, times or prices must be fixed so that PBR [payment by results] workers will earn at least as much as in ... their previous task.... Only these errors ... which favour the worker are acceptable' (NBPI, 1968). For an excellent discussion of piecework bargaining in Britain see Brown, 1973, as well as the NBPI report cited in this footnote.

11 'In most conventional PBR situations, payment for time not on production (in waiting for parts, tools, jigs, inspection and so on) is significantly below the average earnings of the workers concerned so that when management fails to maintain a steady flow of work, it is often the worker rather than the management that is penalized.' This 'acts as a major stimulus to efforts on [the workers'] part to control the payment system's operation' (NBPI, 1968, p.28). Lupton (1963, p.150) gave the same explanation for the attempt by workers at Jay's to 'preserve their area of control' over the pay system there.

12 The failure by supervision to police the reporting of production was another major reason for the breakdown of managerial control, but a discussion of this point is postponed to the next chapter. There the sources of widespread disaffection on the part of supervision are examined.

13 For this point see Brown, 1973; Hunter et al., 1970, p.170.

14 Source: memorandum written by a labor relations manager.

15 For a similar list see OECD, 1970, p.47.

16 'Increases in earnings are inevitably unevenly distributed and thus give rise to pressure for increases elsewhere.... There will be different rates of gain according to the particular circumstances of [workers'] employment, arising from differences in sectional rates of productivity growth, differing institutional arrangements for piece-rate or work-load determination, varying lengths of production run or frequency of changes in task, and so on. Thus inequities and anomalies in relative pay are a frequent and recurring consequence of PBR systems, and these in turn set off pressure for other wage adjustments to bring workers who have fallen behind the leading groups back into line' (NBPI, 1968, p.15).

17 Increases permitted under the incomes policies had to be paid as fixed supplements, i.e., could not be consolidated into piece-rates.

18 'Our findings ... show that [the rate for the job under PBR] is the most common target for pressure to increase earnings over and beyond the provisions of periodic negotiations over basic rates, and presents management with one of the two most difficult problems [the other being differentials between groups of workers] with which it has to deal on a day-to-day basis' (Daniel, 1976, p.34).

19 The minutes of one of the sessions of the 1976-77 annual negotiations included the following exchange:
    The Union said that it is the ongoing no-piecework ... situ-

ation that restricts earning opportunity. This is brought
about by specification changes, Technical Division runs, and
transfers of labour when the employee's own work is available. These all come under 'company convenience.' The hours
attributed to this cause are becoming unreasonable. There is
nothing in the pay policy to say that one cannot bring an
employee back to his rightful earnings position. The employer is to blame for not providing piecework opportunity. The
Union is asking for the removal of the monetary condition of
Job Wage Level [i.e., fixed fallback rates] and replacement
by a percentage of Average Hourly Earnings [which would drift
upwards with piecework earnings] in Sectional Agreement
Areas.

The Management said this is effectively a request for
removal of Sectional Agreements. This would breach the pay
policy since it involves a restructuring.

20   These dangers were not unappreciated when the Labour Government
introduced its pay policy in the 1960s. In 1965 the Ministry of
Labour saw 'one obvious problem' with incomes policy: 'If trade
union leaders accept these wide responsibilities there is a risk
that they will cease to be regarded by their membership as representative of their interests and their influence and authority may be transferred to unofficial leaders.' The employers'
peak association (the CBI) warned that 'restraint by unions in
the official pressing of claims ... [is] calculated to widen
rather than narrow the scope for unofficial action.' The source
for both of these quotations is Panitch, 1976, pp.165-6.

21   In its study of productivity bargaining (NBPI, 1969, p.19), the
Prices and Incomes Board tended to discount this danger: 'On
the other hand there have been other less desirable byproducts.
We found some signs of a feeling, born no doubt of the crude
definition of a productivity agreement as a "sale of restrictive
practices," that cooperation in change now has a cash value and
that it should not be granted too readily.' But there was no
real 'basis for criticism that productivity bargaining gives
rise to an undesirable attitude on the part of workers, who are
tempted to store up restrictive practices which they can later
"sell" in a productivity agreement.'

22   Cf. Lupton (1963, p.168):
Because of the way in which 'booking in' was manipulated, the
records kept by management of worker performance did not represent the way in which time was actually spent.... If
manipulation of booking in is practiced by workers, it follows that management has no accurate record of how time is
spent in a workshop.... And this leads to shortcomings in
scheduling which give rise, in certain conditions, to operatives' attempts to manipulate the incentive system. The
process has a circular form.

23   Cf. Gallie (1978, p.112):
There was no suggestion whatsoever that the source of this
dissatisfaction could best be cured by ... greater worker
participation.... The single most important source of technical criticism concerned maintenance work, but a crucial
feature of this issue was that it pitted one section of the

workforce against the other.... Indeed a good part of the
operators' solution to the problem lay in a much tougher
supervision of maintenance by management. They believed that
the maintenance workers had already achieved too great a
degree of control over the work process, and they wanted an
increase and not a decrease of managerial power. It is very
unlikely, then, that the predominance of technical criticism
in the British refineries is an indication of a desire for
greater control. What is probable is that it reveals that
there is an important area of consensus between management
and workers about the main objectives in running the refinery.... The workers were urging management to do their
job better; they were not seeking to displace management....
An increase in the efficiency of the enterprise was seen ,to
be in the interests of everybody.

24 Source: works council minutes.
25 Compare Kuhn's (1961, p.47) comment: 'Whether the backlog is
high or low, union representatives always complain about it.'
26 See Brown (1973, p.14) on the operation of the 'ratchet effect.'
It may be noted that issuing a provisional rate pending the completion of studies was not a realistic option, even if accompanied by the guarantee that any difference would be made up
retroactively. If set too low the provisional rate would be
rejected by the builders on the grounds that it would remove the
incentive for management to reach a final settlement; conversely, management feared that too generous a provisional rate might
serve as a floor in subsequent negotiations and so protract them
indefinitely.
27 See Table 4.1 where this appears as stoppage No.7.

CHAPTER 6   BREAKDOWN OF GOVERNMENT IN THE WORKPLACE

1 Within the past ten years all of supervision and 60 per cent of
the eligible staff personnel had been organized.
2 Cf. Hartmann, 1959, pp.177-8:
In modern industry the role of the Meister has become problematic. This is due to both technical and administrative
changes. On the technical side increased mechanization has
raised the requirements on technical training in positions of
command.... [Also] the increasing division of functions and
the subversion of line activity by the staff has deprived the
Meister of some of the important functions that he formerly
enjoyed. In Germany, this process is compounded by a far-
reaching legalization of industrial relations. This tends to
take further decisions out of the hands of the Meister and it
demands new specialized knowledge which he does not usually
have at his command.... The evidence from our case studies
suggests that professional management is anxious to improve
the administrative position of the Meister.
Nevertheless, a recent survey of German managers (Fores et al.,
1978, p.88) found that while they 'accept as valid the central
arguments about the loss of functions of foremen, they deny that
any "problem" exists, in the way that Anglo-Saxons see it.'

3   A director of industrial relations told Kuhn (1961, p.18):   'We
    have to keep strings on the foreman, I see no way around it....
    It is important he doesn't give the plant away or put us in con-
    flict with ourselves in grievance settlements.'   According to
    Kuhn the industrial relations department acts as the 'defender
    of the long-run, overall interests of management.   The foremen
    in the shop are not in a position to take over this role, sub-
    ject as they are to the necessities and pressures of daily pro-
    duction in one small section of the plant' (ibid.).   As a result
    'the steps [of the grievance procedure] below the industrial
    relations level are frequently mere formalities' (ibid., p.10).
4   Cf. McCarthy's (1966, pp.30,32) research paper for the Donovan
    Commission: 'Close personal relationships can and do develop
    between shop stewards and plant managers - who may not even know
    the names of all their foremen....   We found that foremen com-
    plained that ... decisions were often taken in negotiations with
    shop stewards about which they were not informed until the
    stewards chose to tell them.'
5   Even before this erosion promotion had not been seen as a paying
    proposition: cf. Goldthorpe (1968, p.123):   'The factor which
    was by far the most important in creating negative attitudes to-
    wards promotion was one which involved economic ... consider-
    ations;   namely, the extent to which supervisory posts were seen
    by our affluent workers as being *disadvantageous* in comparison
    ... with the rank-and-file jobs which they currently occupied.'
6   It is certainly no coincidence that, in the US, it was in war-
    time conditions of acute labor shortages and resultant bargain-
    ing over work standards and piecerates that the Foremen's As-
    sociation of America was founded and mounted a highly successful
    organizing drive.
7   However, in a survey of workers in a German piecework factory,
    Michl (1968, p.137) found that supervisors were the least satis-
    fied with their earnings;   they were on time rates, and in most
    cases they earned less than the operators in their departments.
    It is interesting that the average salary in the English factory
    was fractionally *lower* than the average wage;   in Germany the
    average salary was 143 per cent of the average wage.   However,
    differences in scale and definition mean that these figures must
    be interpreted with great caution.
8   Cf. Slichter et al. (1960, p.824):   'Of course, such a training
    program is useless unless management is willing to support its
    foremen by refusing to overrule them without good reason and by
    refusing to yield to direct pressure tactics from the union.'
9   In the case of the engineers, by two unions.
10 In the British refineries studied by Gallie (1978, p.275) a
    craft/operator differential increase 'brought the first serious
    threat of a strike from the operators.'   'Negotiations with
    management were carried out entirely separately in the two
    cases.   Indeed the separate pattern of negotiations was accompa-
    nied by a certain amount of status rivalry which revealed itself
    in a fairly permanent tension between the two groups about what
    should be the proper differentials between craft and operator
    salaries.'
11 Gallie also reports (1978, p.276) that 'in everyday relations

within the refinery, there appeared to be a minimal degree of cooperation or even of formal contact between the two sets of shop floor representatives....' A branch secretary of the operators' union told Gallie: 'For the last four years I've tried to get meetings between the T&GWU and the Crafts; but I've only once succeeded. There's no real explanation from the crafts why they can't - they just tell us it's not possible.'

12 If plant bargaining is to be successful, according to a Department of Employment study of eleven companies (1971, p.84), it is important that senior stewards have 'considerable strength of character and powers of exposition.'
   In many cases [the chief steward] led a team of shop stewards over which it was essential that he should exert control at the bargaining table. Failure to provide firm leadership meant that a consistent line on union objectives was endangered.... The chief lay official came under greatest pressure. This was especially so where certain sections of the workforce either would fail to benefit, or as was sometimes the case, would actually lose money.

13 McCarthy and Parker (1968, p.72). Compare the statement of one union leader: 'A union executive can guide, it can lead, it can persuade, it can coordinate. What it cannot do is bully or instruct' (Jack Jones in Ferris, 1972).

14 Cf. Flanders (1964, p.140): because of the 'independent authority of the work group ... trade unions may enter agreements which neither they nor management have the power to enforce.... Neither party has sanctions strong enough to override the sanctions of the work group.'

15 'Unions cannot say no to an outstretched hand offering more money' (a trade unionist at a conference on incomes policy, quoted in Blackaby, 1972, p.5). In Germany, the works council would have opposed any pay increases conceded to groups of workers without the council's prior agreement.

16 That this weakness was structural rather than idiosyncratic is supported by Turner et al.'s comment (1967, p.214): 'The chief stewards in car factories are often skilled survivors of long experience of balancing and accommodating these contrary pressures.'

17 For these reasons Donovan (1968, p.130) resisted proposals from the employers' peak association (the CBI) for 'forcing the unions to discipline unofficial strikers.' Such proposals, the Commission said, 'are more likely to lead to internal disruption in the unions than to a reduction in unofficial strikes.'

18 Flanders' comment (1973, p.376) is pertinent here: 'A decayed P.B.R. system can place a very great strain ... on the cohesion and the authority of the body shop stewards. Inequities breed jealousies which are a source of disunity.'

19 In this connection a memorandum from the tire room steward to the Factory Personnel Manager deserves to be quoted in full:
   We, the [labor side of the] Working Party, believe that after consideration of the [Factory Personnel Manager's] letter, it is of a negative nature and does nothing to give us the inducement to conclude a long overdue settlement to the problems of Department ... [i.e., the tire room].

The reference received from us dated 12th July 1977 holds
the key to resolving our differences; the points outlined in
it are short and in a language our members would understand.
The document gives plenty of scope for negotiations that
should ensure a favourable settlement for both parties. We
have used the word 'claim,' you suggest the word 'recommend;'
without embarking on a discourse of words we suggest that at
the end of the day a blend of the two should yield a settlement advantageous to both parties.

We are concerned about the overall Company Working Party's
response to factory-wide job appraisal, and indeed have and
will continue to have the utmost interest in it; but at this
moment of time the position in Department ... continues to
move further into despondency, the situation cries out for
resolvement, the matter is most urgent; we ask for fruitful
talks to continue based on the reference of 12th July 1977,
and a statement of intent issued to Tyre Builders as a News-
letter.

On behalf of the Working Party,
(signed) Representative District....

20 On the basis of his study of ten metalworking factories, Brown
(1973, p.134) has concluded that there are 'four implicit
principles of shop steward behaviour.' These are: (i) Unity;
(ii) equity (which, he says, is interlinked with the first);
(iii) the maintenance of a good bargaining relationship with
management; and (iv) the reduction of uncertainty.

21 The matter would thereby be referred to the next stage of the
company-union grievance procedure.

22 A lifelong socialist, the tire room shop steward laid emphasis
on 'the necessity of discipline for civilized life.' He was
critical of the United States for its inequality; and he said
that he would prefer to live in the USSR ('a disciplined society') than the US ('a sick society'). How far these views reflect working-class authoritarianism and how far the lessons
of the workplace must remain a matter of conjecture.

23 Turner et al., 1967, p.214. Cf. Kuhn's (1960, p.106) description of a shop steward in a US factory where fractional
bargaining was chronic who 'led walkouts, organized slowdowns,
and "cracked down" on foremen not because he thought this was
the best way ... but because he felt he had to guard himself
from the attacks of "hotheads."'

CHAPTER 7   CONCLUSION

1 Doeringer and Piore's well-known study of internal labor markets
in the US suggests that under post-war conditions this has
become an international phenomenon. They say that in 'the
modern industrial economy ... custom tends to grow up around
wage relationships rather than specific wage rates' (1971, p.
85).

2 For a systematic development of this argument see Stephens
(1979).

3 Note that this is not true of Marxist theory per se but simply

of its application in this case, viz. the explanation of industrial disorder as an expression of class conflict.

4   Merton (1968, p.104) points out that these are 'often and
erroneously merged.'

5   Clegg has been taken to task by Shalev (1978; 1980; Korpi and
Shalev, 1979) for his narrowly 'institutional' approach (which
is of course the one I have adopted). Shalev proposes that
strikes and political action be conceptualized as alternative
'working class strategies' in the acting out of class conflict.
When labor has the opportunity to pursue its interests in the
political arena, it renounces the strike weapon: therefore
strikes can be expected to vary inversely with working-class
political power. On close inspection, however, some of the
differences between Clegg and Shalev turn out to be more rhetorical than real. Notably, Shalev reintroduces into his model
certain 'institutional' variables (e.g., a centralized union
movement). While he is at pains to make them out to be no more
than intervening variables, he curiously concedes that they
enjoy a degree of 'functional autonomy' (1980, p.29).

6   The major exception is the horizontally organized DAG (white-
collar union) with a membership of half a million.

7   Cf. 'The Times' (London), 6 February 1978. Under the headline
'Power men poised to form a splinter union' an official of the
shop stewards' national committee is quoted as saying 'The men
feel that the unions are not doing the job. If they fail again
next month the men will not pay their union subscriptions and
will form this breakaway union.'

8   The US has a functional equivalent to this system in its bargaining unit provisions. 'Unions' "responsibility" in regard to
contract observance' has been facilitated by the 'system of exclusive representation within bargaining units. This gives a
union a monopoly position on workers' representation within the
group for which it bargains.... This means that the union is
protected from the defection of members to other unions'
(Garbarino, 1969, p.321).

9   To quote Garbarino (op.cit., p.330) again:
Conflicts within the [bargaining] unit have to be reconciled
within the structure of the employee organization, rather
than appearing as a problem for the employer at separate or
joint bargaining sessions. The union is protected from a
steady attrition of membership over a series of minor
issues.... In the usual case, it appears to permit unions
to accept more responsibility for organizational behavior
than a multi-union situation allows.

10 Garbarino (op.cit., p.321) identified the availability of 'arbitration as an effective alternative' as another factor contributing to American union' responsibility in regard to the observance of agreements.

11 The Conservative Government's Industrial Relations Act (1971)
provided for the first time that a worker under a normal contract of employment could receive compensation for unfair dismissal.

12 See Flanders, 1974, p.353.

13 In Sweden, where industrial unions are the norm, union 'of-

    ficials are reluctant to support members who use the introduction of new machinery to negotiate wage increases. Such negotiations would tend to cause increased differentials and therefore be against union policy' (Pratten, 1976, p.115).

14 For the same point see Kuhn (1961, pp.105-6).

15 For these points see Schmidt, 1972, p.44; Bergmann et al., 1975, p.245; Reichel, 1973, pp.268-9.

16 In 1963 a strike at Daimler-Benz led to a retaliatory lockout of the metal-working industries in the Baden Württemberg region. This was the first lockout of German workers since the 1930s, but its use has become more common in recent years.

17 See for example Beer, 1969, p.360.

18 Garbarino contrasts this with the US's 'relatively high threshold of the economy's and the society's tolerance of industrial conflict' (1969, p.334).

19 E.g., 'last-minute settlements at Downing Street had been a traditional pattern of bargaining on the railways' (Engleman and Thomson, 1974, p.136). For an early case where government pressure undercut a stand taken by employers (with the initial blessing of the Government) see Clegg and Adams (1957). Jackson and Sisson (1976, p.320) draw attention to another factor that has weakened employer solidarity: 'the fact that the state is the largest employer tends to pre-empt any independent initiative by employers in the private sector.'

20 The institutionalization of this process of consultation dates from 1967. It was introduced by the Social Democrat economics minister in the CDU-SPD grand coalition.

APPENDIX THE PERFORMANCE OF THE TWO FACTORIES COMPARED

1 At the start of 1978 the productivity of German industry as a whole was approximately 90 per cent higher than that of British industry (calculated from figures reported in the Dresdner Bank 'Economic Quarterly,' No.58, August 1978). The English factory also compared unfavorably with other European plants. On the basis of a crude comparison of productivity in ten such plants, in only two (one of which was also in the UK) was productivity lower than in the English factory; in another the level was about the same. The German factory had the highest productivity.

2 For a useful discussion see Pratten (1976, ch.1).

3 According to Pratten (1976, p.42), one company reported labor savings of almost 7 per cent after moving to new single-storied premises.

4 Since I did not have access to the factories' financial data it was not possible for me to compute the levels of capital productivity. Nevertheless the fact that the German factory was operating at less than its physical capacity unquestionably meant that the capital employed per production worker was higher in the German factory.

5 Source: minutes of the English factory works council (production workers).

6 Britain's weak trading position is commonly attributed as much

to non-price factors as to lack of price competitiveness. Thus,
it is reported that when a multinational automobile manufacturer
proposed to switch production of a particular model for the
Swedish and Belgian markets to Britain, local dealers strenuous-
ly protested (Central Policy Review Staff, 1975, pp.70-1).

BIBLIOGRAPHY

ALMOND, G. and VERBA, S. (1965), 'The Civic Culture; Political Attitudes and Democracy in Five Nations,' Boston: Little, Brown.
BARKIN, Solomon (1975), 'Worker Militancy and its Consequences, 1965-75; New Directions in Western Industrial Relations,' New York: Praeger.
BEER, Samuel (1958), Group representation in Britain and the United States, 'Annals of the American Academy of Political and Social Science,' vol.319: pp.130-40.
BEER, Samuel (1969), 'British Politics in the Collectivist Age,' New York: Vintage.
BEER, Samuel (1973), Paradoxes of economic power, preface in Stephen Blank, 'Industry and Government in Britain, The Federation of British Industries in Politics, 1945-65,' Farnborough, England: Saxon.
BEHREND, H., LYNCH, H., THOMAS, H. and DAVIES, J. (1967), 'Incomes Policy and the Individual,' Edinburgh: Oliver & Boyd.
BERGMANN, Joachim, JACOBI, O. and MUELLER-JENTSCH, W. (1975), 'Gewerkschaften in der Bundesrepublik,' Frankfurt-Köln: Europäische Verlagsanstalt.
BERGMANN, J. and MUELLER-JENTSCH, W. (1975), The Federal Republic of Germany; cooperative unionism and dual bargaining system challenged, in Solomon Barkin (ed.), 'Worker Militancy and its Consequences: New Directions in Western Industrial Relations,' New York: Praeger.
BLACKABY, Frank (ed.) (1972), 'An Incomes Policy for Britain,' London: Heinemann.
BLANK, Stephen (1979), Britain's economic problems; lies and damn lies, in Isaac Kramnick (ed.), 'Is Britain Dying?.' Ithaca, New York: Cornell.
BLUME, Otto (1956), 'Erfahrungen und Möglichkeiten der Mitbestimmung im Unternehmen,' Tübingen: J.C.B. Mohr.
BROWN, W.A. (1973), 'Piecework Bargaining,' London: Heinemann.
BUTLER, D. and STOKES, D. (1969), 'Political Change in Britain,' New York: St Martin's Press.
CANNON, I.C. (1967), Ideology and occupational community: a study of compositors, 'Sociology,' vol.1: pp.165-85.
CENTRAL POLICY REVIEW STAFF (1975), 'The Future of the British Car Industry,' London: HMSO.

CLEGG, H.A. (1970), 'The System of Industrial Relations in Great Britain,' Oxford: Blackwell.
CLEGG, H.A. (1976), 'Trade Unionism Under Collective Bargaining,' Oxford: Blackwell.
CLEGG, H.A. and ADAMS, Rex (1957), 'The Employer's Challenge,' Oxford: Blackwell.
COLLINS, O., DALTON, M. and ROY, D. (1946), Restriction of output and social cleavage in industry, 'Applied Anthropology,' vol.5: pp.1-14.
COMMISSION ON INDUSTRIAL RELATIONS (1971), Report No.4, 'Birmid Qualcast,' London: HMSO.
COSER, Lewis (1956), 'The Functions of Social Conflict,' Chicago: Free Press.
COTGROVE, S. and VAMPLEW, C. (1972), Technology, class and politics: the case of process workers, 'Sociology,' vol.6, pp.169-85.
COUSINS, Jim (1972), The non-militant shop steward, 'New Society,' February 3.
DAHRENDORF, Ralf (1959), 'Class and Class Conflict in Industrial Society,' Stanford: Stanford University Press.
DAHRENDORF, Ralf (1969), 'Society and Democracy in Germany,' New York: Doubleday (1st German edn 1965).
DANIEL, W.W. (1976), 'Wage Determination in Industry,' London: PEP.
DEPARTMENT OF EMPLOYMENT (1971), 'The Reform of Collective Bargaining at Plant and Company Level,' DE Manpower Papers, No.5, London: HMSO.
DOERINGER, Peter B. and PIORE, Michael J. (1971), 'Internal Labor Markets and Manpower Analysis,' Lexington: Heath.
DONOVAN, Lord (Chairman) (1968), Royal Commission on Trade Unions and Employers' Associations. Report, Cmnd. 3623, London: HMSO.
DUBIN, R. (1954), Constructive aspects of industrial conflict, in A.Kornhauser et al. (eds), 'Industrial Conflict,' New York: McGraw-Hill.
ECKSTEIN, Harry (1962), The British political system, in Samuel Beer and A.B. Ulam (eds), 'Patterns of Government,' 2nd edn, New York: Random House.
EDINGER, Lewis J. (1968), 'Politics in Germany,' Boston: Little, Brown.
ELDRIDGE, J.E.T. (1973), 'Sociology and Industrial Life,' London: Nelson.
ENGLEMAN, S.R. and THOMSON, A.W.J. (1974), Experience under the British Industrial Relations Act, 'Industrial Relations,' vol.13: pp.130-55.
FERRIS, Paul (1972), 'The New Militants: Crisis in the Trade Unions,' Harmondsworth, Middlesex: Penguin.
FLANDERS, Allan (1964), 'The Fawley Productivity Agreements,' London: Faber.
FLANDERS, Allan (1968), 'Trade Unions,' 7th edn, London: Hutchinson.
FLANDERS, Allan (1970), 'Management and Unions,' London: Faber.
FLANDERS, Allan (1973), Measured daywork and collective bargaining, 'British Journal of Industrial Relations,' vol.11: pp.368-92.
FLANDERS, Allan (1974), The tradition of voluntarism, 'British Journal of Industrial Relations,' vol.12: pp.352-70.
FORES, Michael, LAWRENCE, Peter and SORGE, Arndt (1978), Germany's front-line force, 'Management Today,' March: p.87.

FOSH, Patricia and JACKSON, Dudley (1974), Pay policy and inflation: what Britain thinks, 'New Society,' February 7: p.311.

FOX, Alan and FLANDERS, Allan (1970), The reform of collective bargaining. From Donovan to Durkheim, in A.Flanders, 'Management and Unions,' London: Faber.

GALLIE, Duncan (1978), 'In Search of the New Working Class,' Cambridge: Cambridge University Press.

GARBARINO, Joseph W. (1969), Managing conflict in industrial relations, U.S. experience and current issues in Britain, 'British Journal of Industrial Relations,' vol.7: pp.317-35.

GARBARINO, Joseph W. (1973), The British experiment with industrial relations reform, 'Industrial and Labor Relations Review,' vol.26: pp.793-804.

GESTER, Heinz (1972), Zur Stellung der Gewerkschaften im Betrieb nach dem neuen Betriebsverfassungsgesetz, 'Gewerkschaftliche Monatshefte,' vol.23: pp.19-24.

GOLDMAN, Guido (1973), The German political system, in Samuel Beer and A.B. Ulam (eds), 'Patterns of Government,' 3rd edn, New York: Random House.

GOLDTHORPE, John H. (1974a), Social inequality and social integration in modern Britain, in D. Wedderburn, 'Poverty, Inequality and Class Structure,' Cambridge: Cambridge University Press.

GOLDTHORPE, John H. (1974b), Industrial relations in Britain: A critique of reformism, 'Politics and Society,' vol.4, pp.419-52.

GOLDTHORPE, John H. (1978), The current inflation: Towards a sociological account, in Fred Hirsch and John Goldthorpe, 'The Political Economy of Inflation,' Cambridge, Mass.: Harvard.

GOLDTHORPE, John J., LOCKWOOD, D., BECHHOFER, F. and PLATT, J. (1968), 'The Affluent Worker: Industrial Attitudes and Behaviour,' Cambridge: Cambridge University Press.

GOODMAN, J.F.B. and WHITTINGHAM, T.G. (1969), 'Shop Stewards in British Industry,' Maidenhead: McGraw-Hill.

HARDIN, Garrett (1968), The tragedy of the commons, 'Science,' vol. 162: pp.1243-8.

HARTMANN, Heinz (1959), 'Authority and Organization in German Management,' Princeton: Princeton University Press.

HAWKINS, Kevin (1976), 'British Industrial Relations, 1974-75,' London: Barrie & Jenkins.

HIRSCH, Fred (1978), 'Social Limits to Growth,' Cambridge, Mass.: Harvard University Press.

HUNTER, L.C., REID, G.L. and BODDY, D. (1970), 'Labour Problems of Technological Change,' London: George Allen & Unwin.

HYMAN, Richard and BROUGH, Ian (1975), 'Social Values and Industrial Relations,' Oxford: Blackwell.

INGHAM, Geoffrey K. (1970), 'Size of Industrial Organization and Workplace Behaviour,' Cambridge: Cambridge University Press.

INGHAM, Geoffrey K. (1974), 'Strikes and Industrial Conflict,' London: Macmillan.

JACKSON, Peter and SISSON, Keith (1976), Employers' confederations in Sweden and the U.K. and the significance of industrial infrastructure, 'British Journal of Industrial Relations,' vol.14: pp.306-23.

JAY, Peter (1976), 'Employment, Inflation and Politics,' London: Institute of Economic Affairs.

JENSEN, Vernon H. (1971), 'Decasualization and Modernization of Dock Work in London,' Ithaca, New York: New York State School of Industrial and Labor Relations, Cornell University.
KERR, Clark (1954), The trade union movement and the redistribution of power in postwar Germany, 'Quarterly Journal of Economics,' vol.68: pp.535-64.
KERR, Clark (1957), Collective bargaining in postwar Germany, in A. Sturmthal (ed.), 'Contemporary Collective Bargaining in Seven Countries,' Ithaca, New York: New York State School of Industrial and Labor Relations, Cornell University.
KILPATRICK, Andrew and LAWSON, Tony (1980), On the nature of industrial decline in the UK, 'Cambridge Journal of Economics,' vol. 4: pp.85-102.
KORPI, Walter and SHALEV, Michael (1979), Strikes, industrial relations and class conflict in capitalist societies, 'British Journal of Sociology,' vol.30: pp.164-87.
KUHN, James W. (1961), 'Bargaining in Grievance Settlement,' New York: Columbia University Press.
LANE, Tony and ROBERTS, Kenneth (1971), 'Strike at Pilkingtons,' London: Fontana.
LATTA, Geoff (1972), Trade union finance, 'British Journal of Industrial Relations,' vol.10: pp.392-411.
LEMINSKY, Gerhard (1975), Probleme der Betriebsverfassung, 'Gewerkschaftliche Monatshefte,' vol.26: pp.585-9.
LINDBLOM, Charles (1959), The science of 'muddling through', 'Public Administration Review,' vol.19: pp.79-88.
LIPSET, Seymour Martin (1963), 'Political Man,' New York: Anchor.
LUPTON, Tom (1963), 'On the Shop Floor,' London: Pergamon.
McBEATH, Innis (1973), 'The European Approach to Worker-Management Relationships,' London and Washington, D.C.: British-North American Committee.
McCARTHY, W.E.J. (1966), 'The Role of Shop Stewards in British Industrial Relations,' Royal Commission research paper 1, London: HMSO.
McCARTHY, W.E.J. and PARKER, S.R. (1968), 'Shop Stewards and Workshop Relations,' Royal Commission research paper 10, London: HMSO.
McKENZIE, R.T. and SILVER, Allan (1968), 'Angels in Marble: Working Class Conservatives in Urban England,' London: Heinemann.
MANN, Michael (1970), The social cohesion of liberal democracy, 'American Sociological Review,' vol.35: pp.423-39.
MANN, Michael (1973), 'Consciousness and Action among the Western Working Class,' London: Macmillan.
MEHRLÄNDER, Ursula (1974), 'Soziale Aspekte der Ausländer-beschäftigung,' Bonn-Bad Godesberg: Verlag Neue Gesellschaft.
MELMAN, Seymour (1958), 'Decision-Making and Productivity,' Oxford: Blackwell.
MERTON, Robert K. (1968), 'Social Theory and Social Structure,' New York: Free Press.
MICHL, Alfred W. (1968), 'Entlohnungssysteme und sozialer Konflikt,' Berlin: Duncker & Humblot.
MORAN, Michael (1977), 'The Politics of Industrial Relations: The Origins, Life and Death of the 1971 Industrial Relations Act,' London: Macmillan.

NATIONAL BOARD FOR PRICES AND INCOMES (1968), 'Payment by Results Systems,' London: HMSO.
NATIONAL BOARD FOR PRICES AND INCOMES (1969), 'Productivity Agreements,' London: HMSO.
NICKEL, W. (1978), Zum Image der Gewerkschaften, 'Gewerkschaftliche Monatshefte,' vol.29: p.232.
OLSON, Mancur (1971), 'The Logic of Collective Action,' Cambridge, Mass.: Harvard University Press.
ORGANIZATION FOR ECONOMIC COOPERATION AND DEVELOPMENT (1970), 'Forms of Wage and Salary Payment for High Productivity,' Final Report, Paris: OECD.
PANIC, Misha (1976), 'The UK and West German Manufacturing Industry 1954-72,' NEDO, London: HMSO.
PANITCH, Leo (1976), 'Social Democracy and Industrial Militancy,' New York: Cambridge University Press.
PANITCH, Leo (1979), The development of corporatism in liberal democracies, in Philippe C.Schmitter and Gerhard Lehmbruch (eds), 'Trends Toward Corporatist Intermediation,' Beverly Hills, California: Sage.
PARKER, Stanley (1973), 'Workplace Industrial Relations,' London: HMSO.
PARKIN, Frank (1972), 'Class, Inequality and Political Order,' London: Paladin.
PARSONS, Talcott (1957), The distribution of power in American society, 'World Politics,' vol.10: pp.123-43.
PARSONS, Talcott (1968), 'The Structure of Social Action,' New York: Free Press.
POPPER, Karl R. (1971), 'The Open Society and Its Enemies,' vol.2, Princeton, New Jersey: Princeton University Press (originally published 1962).
PRATTEN, C.F. (1976), 'Labour Productivity Differentials Within International Companies,' Cambridge: Cambridge University Press.
PRATTEN, C.F. (1977), 'A Comparison of the Performance of Swedish and U.K. Companies,' Cambridge: Cambridge University Press.
REICHEL, Hans (1973), Recent trends in collective bargaining in the Federal Republic of Germany, in 'Collective Bargaining in Industrialized Market Economies,' Geneva: ILO.
ROBERTI, Paolo (1978), Income inequality in some Western Countries: patterns and trends, 'International Journal of Social Economics,' vol.5: p.22.
ROETHLISBERGER, Fritz J. (1945), The foreman: master and victim of doubletalk, 'Harvard Business Review,' vol.23: pp.283-98.
ROGALY, Joe (1977), 'Grunwick,' Harmondsworth, Middlesex: Penguin.
ROSE, Richard (1964), 'Politics in England,' Boston: Little, Brown.
ROSS, Arthur M. (1962), Prosperity and labor relations in Europe: the case of West Germany, 'Quarterly Journal of Economics,' vol.76: pp.331-60.
ROY, Donald (1955), Efficiency and 'the Fix'; informal intergroup relations in a piecework machine shop, 'American Journal of Sociology,' vol.60: pp.255-66.
ROYAL COMMISSION ON TRADE UNIONS AND EMPLOYERS' ASSOCIATIONS (Donovan Report) (1968), Cmnd. 3623, London: HMSO.
RUNCIMAN, W.G. (1966), 'Relative Deprivation and Social Justice; A Study of Attitudes to Social Inequality in Twentieth Century England,' Berkeley: University of California Press.

SAWYER, Malcolm (1976), Income distribution in OECD countries, 'OECD Occasional Studies,' Paris: OECD.
SAYLES, Leonard R. (1958), 'Behavior of Industrial Work Groups: Prediction and Control,' New York: Wiley.
SCASE, Richard (1974), Relative deprivation: a comparison of English and Swedish manual workers, in D. Wedderburn (ed.), 'Poverty, Inequality and Class Structure,' Cambridge: Cambridge University Press.
SCASE, Richard (1977), 'Social Democracy in Capitalist Society,' London: Rowman and Littlefield.
SCHELLING, Thomas C. (1973), 'The Strategy of Conflict,' London and New York: Oxford University Press.
SCHELLING, Thomas C. (1974), On the ecology of micromotives, in Robin Marris (ed.), 'The Corporate Society,' New York: Wiley.
SCHMIDT, Folke (1972), Industrial action: the role of trade unions and employers' associations, in B. Aaron and K.W. Wedderburn (eds), 'Industrial Conflict,' New York: Crane, Russak.
SCHMIEDE, R. and SCHUDLICH, E. (1976), 'Die Entwicklung der Leistungsentlohnung in Deutschland,' Frankfurt: Aspekte Verlag.
SCHNEIDER, Wolfgang (1975), Betriebsratswahlen 1975 - eine zusammen-fassende Darstellung, 'Gewerkschaftliche Monatshefte,' vol.26: pp. 600-7.
SHALEV, Michael (1978), Strikers and the state: a comment, 'British Journal of Political Science,' vol.8: pp.479-92.
SHALEV, Michael (1980), Industrial relations theory and the comparative study of industrial relations and industrial conflict, 'British Journal of Industrial Relations,' vol.18: pp.29-43.
SLICHTER, S.H., HEALY, J.J. and LIVERNASH, E.R. (1960), 'The Impact of Collective Bargaining on Management,' Washington, D.C.: Brookings.
SPIRO, Herbert J. (1958), 'The Politics of German Codetermination,' Cambridge, Mass.: Harvard University Press.
SPIRO, Herbert J. (1962), The German political system, in Samuel Beer and A.B. Ulam (eds), 'Patterns of Government,' 2nd edn, New York: Random House.
STEPHENS, John D. (1979), Class formation and class consciousness; theoretical and empirical analysis with reference to Britain and Sweden, 'British Journal of Sociology,' vol.30: pp.389-414.
STREECK, Wolfgang (1981), Qualitative demands and neo-corporatist manageability of industrial relations, 'British Journal of Industrial Relations,' vol.19: pp.149-69.
STURMTHAL, Adolf (1964), 'Workers Councils,' Cambridge, Mass.: Harvard University Press.
TOURAINE, Alain and RAGAZZI, O. (1961), 'Ouvriers d'origine agricole,' Paris: Editions du Seuil.
TURNER, H.A., CLACK, G. and ROBERTS, G. (1967), 'Labour Relations in the Motor Industry,' London: George Allen & Unwin.
WEBER, Max (1946), 'From Max Weber,' H.H. Gerth and C. Wright Mills (eds), New York: Oxford University Press.
WEDDERBURN, D. and CROMPTON, R. (1972), 'Workers' Attitudes and Technology,' Cambridge: Cambridge University Press.
WEEKES, Brian, MELLISH, Michael, DICKENS, Linda and LLOYD, John (1975), 'Industrial Relations and the Limits of Law,' Oxford: Blackwell.

WITLEY, Richard J. (1974), Trade unions and political parties in the Federal Republic of Germany, 'Industrial and Labor Relations Review,' vol.28:   pp.38-59.
WOODWARD, Joan (1958), 'Management and Technology,' London: HMSO.
ZACHERT, Ulrich (1978), Aussperrung und Gewerkschaften, 'Gewerkschaftliche Monatshefte,' vol.29:   p.280.

INDEX